In *The Path to Wholeness*, Dr. Mark Mayfield [...] their feelings, emotions, and relationships to [...] lives. I highly recommend it.

> **DANIEL G. AMEN, MD,** founder of Amen Clinics and author of
> *Change Your Brain Every Day*

Emotions are often seen as a problem for our lives. Especially when our emotions are painful, we don't trust them and try to avoid them. Yet, as Dr. Mayfield explains, emotions are a blessing from God when we face, understand, express, and mature them. This process offers a significant contribution for our lives and growth.

> **JOHN TOWNSEND, PhD,** psychologist, author of the *New York Times*–
> bestselling Boundaries book series, and founder of the Townsend Institute
> and Townsend Leadership Program

In the book you are holding, Dr. Mark Mayfield writes in a transparent and vulnerable manner, sharing from his clinical experiences and from his personal journey. We both found this book not only loaded with insight but also rich with application for readers. Do more than read this book— digest it, take notes, and pass it on to others who are thirsty to understand more of what a journey to wholeness offers.

> **DR. GARY AND BARB ROSBERG,** authors, speakers, and marriage coaches
> at The Rosberg Group and America's Family Coaches

Language is a structured system of communication. Imagine, though, living your whole life being told that your mother tongue, the one that you speak most readily, is nonsense. Imagine, also, what it might mean to meet someone who not only believes that language to be valuable but also speaks it so fluently that your entire being cries out with relief. Our emotions are that language, and many inside and outside the church have been taught that it is worse than nonsense. In *The Path to Wholeness*, Dr. Mark Mayfield gives readers back the language they spoke with ease as young children and often feel deeply alienated from as adults. And in so doing, he has paved a path to healing for many.

> **TARA M. OWENS, CSD, CSDS,** spiritual director, supervisor, and executive
> director of Anam Cara Ministries; author of *Embracing the Body*

Managing emotions. Finding healing. Becoming our best selves. Those aren't just the small-print words on the cover. They are the deep takeaways I believe you'll gain from reading this insightful, extremely honest, hope-filled, and faith-strengthening book. I've met Dr. Mayfield. Heard him impact and inspire large groups. *But this book is personal.* And I think it can be incredibly helpful to you at a deep, personal level. Especially if, like me, you need to gain wisdom in dealing with emotions. If you're ready to learn skills that can give you a genuine path out of fear, anxiety, and shame. And if you're ready to believe you can rewrite and live out a new narrative for your life story.

JOHN TRENT, PhD, president of StrongFamilies.com and coauthor of *The Blessing* and *Where Do I Go from Here?*

Dr. Mark Mayfield has given us a rich combination of brain science, trauma awareness, attachment theory, and related theology to help us understand our own emotional landscape. *The Path to Wholeness* provides language and guidance that will help readers know the steps to move forward in their own healing. Mayfield's wisdom is compassionately given from the perspective of someone who is genuinely journeying along with his readers.

JANICE McWILLIAMS, MDiv, LCPC, author of *Restore My Soul*

THE

MANAGING EMOTIONS,

PATH TO

FINDING HEALING, AND BECOMING

WHOLENESS

OUR BEST SELVES

DR. MARK MAYFIELD

A NavPress resource published in alliance
with Tyndale House Publishers

NavPress is the publishing ministry of The Navigators, an international Christian organization and leader in personal spiritual development. NavPress is committed to helping people grow spiritually and enjoy lives of meaning and hope through personal and group resources that are biblically rooted, culturally relevant, and highly practical.

For more information, visit NavPress.com.

The Path to Wholeness: Managing Emotions, Finding Healing, and Becoming Our Best Selves

A NavPress resource published in alliance with Tyndale House Publishers

NavPress and the NavPress logo are registered trademarks of NavPress, The Navigators, Colorado Springs, CO. *Tyndale* is a registered trademark of Tyndale House Ministries. Absence of ® in connection with marks of NavPress or other parties does not indicate an absence of registration of those marks.

The Team:
David Zimmerman, Publisher; Deborah Sáenz Gonzalez, Acquisitions Editor; Deborah Howell, Copy Editor; Olivia Eldredge, Operations Manager; Ron Kaufmann, Designer; Sarah K. Johnson, Proofreader

Cover illustration of landscape copyright © Andy Vinnikov/depositphotos.com. All rights reserved.

Author photo by Rachael Hendrickson, copyright © 2022. All rights reserved.

For information about special discounts for bulk purchases, please contact Tyndale House Publishers at csresponse@tyndale.com, or call 1-855-277-9400.

ISBN 978-1-64158-531-6

Printed in the United States of America

29	28	27	26	25	24	23
7	6	5	4	3	2	1

To Hannah, Elizabeth, and August.
It is my greatest joy to be your dad. I pray that the message
of this book and my own path toward wholeness have a
lasting impact on you and the generations to come.
I love you!

CONTENTS

FOREWORD

IT'S BEEN A ROUGH ROAD THE LAST COUPLE OF YEARS
. . . for everyone. I have been sharing a lot lately how prior to the
COVID-19 pandemic, we had a mental-health crisis in America
and around the world. Since then, with lockdowns, loss, and
loneliness; racial trauma; tension and rioting; the election mess;
the race for a vaccine; the rollout; variants; tensions and war
around the globe; shootings; and more, it was only intuitive to
know that we would see a serious spike in mental health–related
issues. And we have. We've seen increased stress and anxiety, and
fear is dominating our culture. Depression, addiction, and even
suicidality is soaring . . . even among our kids.

The bottom line: People are exhausted and emotionally shot.
Traumatized. As a matter of fact, one of the big themes at recent
Christian counseling events has been collective trauma. People
everywhere are shell-shocked, hurting, confused, angry, and
searching frantically for help, hope, and encouragement.

What is encouraging is that people are still looking to God and
to faith-based mental-health and ministry leaders, and they want
their faith addressed as part of the healing journey.

One thing is clear to me: We don't need God less; we need him more in such a time as this. Especially in the counseling office.

Enter Dr. Mark Mayfield. Mark has been on a journey since he was a boy to find emotional freedom and peace. He knows brokenness and pain. Darkness. And light. He has found hope and healing.

Since then, God has taken Mark down numerous paths to equip and train him to speak and give words of life to others. And he has developed a strong, bold, and hopeful voice. The work you now hold in your hands, *The Path to Wholeness*, offers clarity and focused direction on pressing though challenging and confusing past emotions, current chaos, and toxic issues and paves a road to emotional freedom.

Anchored in a heart for God and filled with clinical wisdom, this book is a traveler's gift.

May God work in and through you as you read and apply its content and then continue on the road forward.

Dr. Tim Clinton
president of the American Association of Christian Counselors and executive director of Liberty University's Global Center for Mental Health, Addiction, and Recovery

Part One

EMOTIONS DEVELOPED

1

THE NEED FOR LANGUAGE

"Your emotions make you human. . . .
Even the unpleasant ones have a purpose.
Don't lock them away. If you ignore them,
they just get louder and angrier."
SABAA TAHIR, *A Torch against the Night*

Definitions
Emotions: The psychological states brought on by a neuro-physiological change associated with thoughts, experiences, and behavioral responses, with a degree of pleasure or displeasure.

Feelings: The perceptions of events within the body (the conscious experience of emotional reactions) and the intentional choice to make meaning from those perceptions using language and past experiences.

Principles: "Fundamental truth[s] or proposition[s] that [serve] as the foundation for a system of belief or behavior or for a chain of reasoning";[1] basic or general truths on which other units or traits can be based.

AMY'S BODY LANGUAGE SAID IT ALL. She sat on the couch across from Tim, slightly turned toward the door, arms folded and lips pursed. It was as if she was either trying really hard to keep a secret or doing everything she could not to explode.

The energy in my office was tense. I could feel it, and my stomach was agreeing with me as it did somersaults. Amy was upset, and the whole room knew it. Tim had chosen to sit in an armchair on the other side of the room, away from Amy. His body language also communicated everything. He was lost and defeated. He sat with one leg propped up on the seat and the other dangling off. His arms wrapped around his leg as he brought it close to his chest. He was hurt, and he was trying hard to protect himself. Amy and Tim had been coming to me for couples counseling for nearly three months. We had been working hard to uncover the layers of hurt and misunderstanding that had built up over their fifteen years of marriage.

I cleared my throat and said, "I find it interesting that you chose to sit in separate spaces today. Usually you sit on the couch together and attempt to show that you love each other. Today it feels like the veil is lifted, and I am finally experiencing the real you." I paused and looked at Amy and Tim. Amy caught my gaze and quickly looked away. Tim didn't even bother looking up. I let the silence linger. By this time, the tension in the room was palpable. I felt it, and they felt it, too, as they shifted and squirmed in their seats.

Finally, Tim said, "What's the point of this? We are never going to be on the same page."

Amy huffed and contorted her body even more toward the door as if she were getting ready to run. "Tim," I quietly said, "can you expand a bit more? I have a hard time believing you are ready to throw away fifteen years of marriage."

Tim sat up straight in his chair, looked at me with some intensity, and said, "You are right! I don't want to give up! But we are speaking two different languages. I don't know how to get through to her." With those words barely trailing off his lips, Amy turned around and squared off with Tim.

"Exactly!" she shouted. "We are speaking two different languages. Someone needs to translate for us."

I will never forget that exchange. It was heated, it was emotional, and it defused the tensions. They were starting to talk to each other instead of at each other. They were starting to get to the root cause of their turmoil.

We spent the next hour and then subsequent weeks unpacking and exploring that exchange. As things became clearer, it was evident that Amy and Tim each thought they were communicating clearly, and in some ways they were, but their definitions, their language, and their experiences around what they were attempting to communicate were entirely different. The result was that they were missing each other on all levels. Their struggle centered around their internal and external understanding of intimacy. Tim saw intimacy through the lens of relationship, quality time, and service to his wife. Amy saw intimacy as physical touch that could lead to sex. For years, they were using the same word to communicate completely different ideas.

Can you relate to Amy and Tim? I know I can. My wife, Sarah, and I had a similar argument early in our marriage, and we struggled to work through it. This is one reason I chose to write a book on emotions. It is clear to me that we are somehow missing the mark.

We are missing the mark in how we talk and teach about emotions in our society, our school systems, and our churches. We are missing the mark in how we help people navigate emotional turmoil. Despite the wealth of information available about emotional and mental wellness, some people will never gain access to it. We have a systemic problem that needs to be addressed.

Everyone, regardless of education level, socioeconomic status, religion, and so on, should have equal access to information about mental and emotional health. In case you can't tell, this is something I am very passionate about. I don't like creating a system where there are "haves" and "have-nots," but many times this is what the education system does, and to some degree, what the mental-health field does. I want to demystify these topics and make them accessible to everyone.

In New Testament times, there was a group of religious people called the Gnostics. The Gnostics believed they had secret knowledge about heaven that no one else had access to. Sometimes I feel that way about academia and the mental-health field. We have our theories, our research, and our information, but we don't readily simplify and translate it to be consumed by the masses. I want these concepts about emotional and mental wellness to not only reach your cognitive mind but also to reach your emotional mind. I want you to mull over these concepts, ruminate on them, wrestle with them, and then integrate them into the fabric of who you are.

Waves and Emotions

Waves are hypnotic, rhythmic, wild, and dangerous. To an experienced beachgoer, the waves are a predictable friend, welcome and calming. But to someone who hasn't spent time near the ocean, they can be terrifying and unpredictable. How can the same waves have two different effects? Perspective and experience. If that is true, how does someone gain perspective and experience? The answer is time and exposure. Emotions are the same way. For one person, they are a welcome interaction; for another, they are terrifying. Same emotion, different perspective, different experiences. Is one right and the other wrong?

Have you ever stopped to consider what an emotion is? I mean really putting some thought into it. Most people don't have a good answer to this question, which surprises me. I have devoted my life to the study of the human condition. I sit with people on a daily basis, helping them make sense of this messed-up world, and often, their messed-up life within it. I teach coping skills, breathing techniques, and mindfulness exercises. I help people make sense of their pasts, their childhoods, and their trauma. I've been trained in cognitive behavioral therapy, eye movement desensitization reprocessing therapy, and many other areas, but if someone were to ask me to succinctly define what emotions are and how they originate, I am not even sure how I would answer that. How would you answer?

This sparked my interest, and I wondered why I wasn't specifically taught this in my master's or doctorate counseling programs. As I began to ponder the classes I took, and now, the classes I teach at Colorado Christian University, I've come to realize that such courses assume we all know what emotions are and how they fundamentally operate. I sat with this realization for a couple of days, and as I did, I became more and more disturbed. Why? We'd been thinking we'd been speaking the same language, using the same nouns, verbs, and adjectives to describe our experiences, our stories, and our narratives, when in essence, we had been completely missing each other. I then began to wonder what other factors were contributing to this catastrophic misunderstanding:

- **Psychological expectations get in the way of effective communication.** What are psychological expectations? Typically, these are the "shoulds" in a relationship. For example, my wife *should* know that when I get home from a long day at work I need twenty minutes to decompress before I engage with the family. Or my daughters *should* know the rules of respect in the home and not talk back to their mom or me. The problems start when these "shoulds" are not fully communicated or clearly understood by the entire family.

  It is the same with emotions. We are communicating constantly, but only 10 percent of what we communicate is verbal, which means that 90 percent is nonverbal. And between 50 and 75 percent of the nonverbal is the psychological (unspoken and assumed) "should"! This means we assume that others have the same perspective on and understanding of our emotions as we do. Moreover, we often have different interpretations of what is being communicated versus what is being received. If this remains in the unspoken psychological realm, we will constantly be frustrated and discouraged. I will talk later in this book about the remedy to this problem.

- **We all had different experiential models, so we all have different starting points.** Think about it. Where did you learn about emotions? Most of us learned from our early relational models—our moms, dads, aunts, uncles, grandparents, siblings, teachers, and friends. Just like psychological expectations, much of our learning came from observation and our own conscious or unconscious interpretation of that observation. We watched those closest to us, we saw how they responded to events, to their spouses, to stress, and we made mental models of what we saw. Eventually those models became our own. For example, I struggle with using tone when I communicate. It could just be because I have a streak of Italian in me, or it could be because of what I observed growing up. When I am upset or frustrated, I can sound mean and condescending to my wife and children. I have been working on reversing this for the past fifteen years and am getting better, but where did I learn it? I did not wake up one morning and think, *I'm going to use a mean, sarcastic, and condescending tone with my wife and kids so that I can hurt their feelings.* I learned it specifically from watching my dad and grandfather. Now, before you get upset with me for "outing" my family: My dad and I have talked through this at length, and he, too, has made significant strides to change. I remember one conversation he and I had where he disclosed that he had learned how to communicate by watching his dad, and he confessed that "at least I wasn't as bad as he was."

Can you start to see how complicated this can become? For many of us, generational patterns are unintentionally passed on, and until we become aware of these patterns, we are unable to make the necessary changes. Unfortunately, there isn't a how-to book for this. We try our best, we do "better" than our parents, and we do what we can not to mess up our families. It is a sobering fact that my kids are watching and observing me, and I have to be very intentional about what models I am passing down to them.

- **We lack shared vocabulary, further complicating communication.** I always say that language creates culture and culture creates direction. Far too often, I've found, there is a lack of emotional vocabulary in our culture. *Mad, sad,* and *glad* are about as far as many of us get. So when we are faced with complex emotions, we feel lost, confused, and unable to speak the necessary language. To make matters worse, we may think we are speaking the same or "right" language, but we are actually saying something completely different. Not only does language create culture—it can also create mutual understanding through shared experiences or commonality.

Emotional Immaturity

"You are so immature!" Kylee yelled from across the playground. "Grow up!" I shouted back. "You're the one who's immature!" The exchange went back and forth a couple more times, and then we parted ways. Reflecting on that memory, I smile, because I've forgotten why we were so upset with each other. It was probably something to do with "girls have cooties and boys drool," and we became incensed by those comments and began the frivolous exchange. We were in second grade, and we were emotionally immature. Has anything really changed as we've gotten older? Maybe we've become more sophisticated in our banter, but the underlying message is still similar to that second-grade exchange.

Have you noticed? We are an emotionally driven society. We often react before we think. We respond with how we feel, or at least how we think we feel. But what if the majority of us are getting it wrong? We believe our emotions to be true because that's how we "feel" in the moment. But with added context and awareness, we realize we're getting it all wrong.

As I was exploring this thought, I began to question anything and everything I've been taught about emotions—about pain, joy, suffering, contentment, excitement, peace, and so on. What if for generations we've been (albeit while doing the best we can) teaching and emulating the wrong things? What if there is a better way to engage and interact with our emotions that can make us a deeper, more seasoned society? What if the relearning of our emotions and our emotional experiences could actually create greater unity rather than widening the divide of tribalism? I'm not promising this—I'm just intrigued by the possibility.

Emotions are neither good nor bad; they just are. I need you to reread that and let it sink in. When we are quick to label something as good, the assumption is that the other side of the spectrum is bad. So if joy is good, then sadness is bad. We see this type of logic played out all over our society. *Raiders football team bad, Broncos football team good. Republicans bad, Democrats good. Evangelicals good*... Why is this? For one thing, it is human nature. Our brains and psyches believe they can only handle black-and-white thinking. But in actuality, the lack of complexity actually slows down the brain's growth and functioning.

Thought Generator: Creating an Emotional Backlog

I don't know about you, but I often have thoughts swirling around in my head. Most of the time they are truly random: *What did I have for dinner last night? Did I turn the light off in the bathroom? Why did that guy look at me like that yesterday—did I have something on my face?* My wife often jokes that I don't have a turn signal and tend to jump from one thought to another. She's right, but the jumps make complete sense to me! Maybe you can relate. Our brains can generate up to fifty thousand thoughts a day. That is a lot of randomness. But many times, my thoughts are not random and can spiral into toxic or negative patterns. This is often the case with the negative stories we've told ourselves or heard from others our whole lives.

The story that was repeated throughout my life was that I was an awkward loser who was oversensitive. Though I have done extensive work in this area of my life, that story can creep in at odd or unannounced times. If it were just a thought or a series of thoughts, it wouldn't be that big a deal, but there is always, and I mean always, an emotion that goes with it. This is a key component that is often missed in this conversation, and it makes all the difference. Why? When we miss the emotion attached to a thought, we begin to stack the emotion like a teetering Jenga game. When that emotion is not recognized and processed, it stays, and then the next emotion experienced is stacked on the previous one until the tower falls, creating a cascading avalanche of emotions. It is like a toddler mixing all the Play-Doh colors into one brown mess. If we had simply recognized and processed the original emotion, the entire catastrophe could have been avoided.

Purpose of This Book
This book is written for you, and it is written for me. It is an intentional wrestling with a concept that "should" be common sense and "should" be easy but isn't. Emotions are confusing, frustrating, and scary, but they don't have to be. It is my desire that you slow down and explore each concept in this book. Yes, the concepts are broken up into distinct chapters, but they intersect on many different levels.

Each chapter will start with definitions so that we can create common language. Then I will share principles that will guide the conversation. Finally, at the end of each chapter, I will provide questions for reflection and specific action steps.

I will ask you to look inward at your own experience and your own history. I will ask you to reflect on how these things have shaped, informed, and influenced you, your family, and your relationships. I will challenge you to dissect your current understanding of emotions, your emotional vocabulary, and your emotional responses. Then I will provide practical and actionable steps to rethink and rework how you see and experience emotions. If you take the time and slow down, this book can and will be transformational for you and those around you. Why? Because this practice forces you to stop, sit with, and reflect on your internal status, and when you genuinely do this, you will be compelled to action—and eventually, to change. So I invite you to join me on this journey. Pull out a new journal and unwrap a new pen; take notes; write down your thoughts, feelings, and emotions, and let's embark on this path together.

Questions for Reflection

1. How would you describe your emotional vocabulary?

2. What has been your experience with emotions throughout your life?

3. How would you rate your emotional intelligence?

4. What emotion has been most uncomfortable for you? Why?

Action Steps

In your journal, write out your most pervasive emotion. Track it this week and see how often it pops up and what circumstances surround it.

WHY MODELS MATTER

And mothers are their daughters' role model,
their biological and emotional road map,
the arbiter of all their relationships.

VICTORIA SECUNDA

Definitions

Model: "A system or thing used as an example to follow or imitate."[1]

Neurons: "The fundamental units of the brain and nervous system, the cells responsible for receiving sensory input from the external world, for sending motor commands to our muscles, and for transforming and relaying the electrical signals at every step in between."[2]

SEVERAL YEARS AGO, I worked with a young man named Alex. He was referred to me by his youth pastor. Alex was almost sixteen years old; he was over six feet tall and had an athletic build. Until recently, Alex had been a straight-A student and the captain of his baseball team. In recent months, his grades had slipped, and he had become more "reactive" at school and church. The straw that had broken the camel's back was his most recent outburst at church.

According to his youth pastor, Alex was taking part in a youth-leadership activity when someone made a comment about how Alex responded to something. The youth pastor stated, "It was like he changed into a completely different person. One minute, he was fine; the next minute, he got red in the face, yelled at us, and stormed off to the restroom." He continued, "I ran after him and found him in the bathroom, sitting on the floor, knees up to his chest, embarrassed and crying."

It took several sessions for Alex to open up to me, but when he did, he began to verbalize what was going on. He had no real model for emotional processing, communication, or expression. He'd grown up in a stable home. Both of his parents were active in the church, his dad showed up to every baseball game, and his mom consistently supported him in his education. They were present but not engaged. His dad was an engineer, and his mom was a law clerk. They provided well for the family, but there was a piece missing.

I asked Alex to describe what emotions looked like in his home. He just looked at me with a blank stare. I pressed. "When someone gets upset, how do they express themselves? Is there yelling? What kind of tone? Are there tears? What happens, and how is it resolved?"

"Um, I'm not sure," he quietly responded.

"Not sure?" I said. "What do you mean?"

"Well, I've never actually seen my parents upset with each other, and when I start to get upset myself, I'm told to go to my room until I'm not emotional anymore."

The more we unpacked his story, the more I realized he truly had no frame of reference for how to process or communicate his emotions. Several weeks after we made this realization in a session, Alex built up the courage to invite his parents into his counseling. He was worried that they would get defensive, and he didn't want to make matters worse. All he wanted was to open up his communication with them and deepen their relationship. We spent some time practicing his conversations until he felt comfortable. The day came for his parents to join, and the outcome surprised us both. Instead of defensiveness and anger, Alex received compassion and tears. I watched Alex as his parents responded, and I could see layers of walls start to break down. Both of Alex's parents conveyed the fact that they hadn't had any emotional or relational models in their childhood homes. In fact, they were happy that they were doing better than their parents. The problem was that there wasn't any communication or common language in their home to test how they were actually doing. The cool thing about this story is that Alex's parents requested individual counseling and family counseling so that they could begin to heal and explore their own narratives, break generational wounds, and develop a more thoughtful and intentional language at home.

Maybe you can relate to Alex's story. This is an all-too-common scenario. Maybe you saw your parents be "overexpressive," with every emotional discussion becoming an argument. Maybe your mom used a certain tone when she talked to you and now you struggle with tone. Maybe your dad became silent and would storm out when things got tough. Whatever the situation may be, the point is this: Most of how we process, communicate, or express our emotions comes from the models in our lives.

I don't want this realization to be a blaming session. Most people do the best they can with what they were taught growing up. Until you are provided with an alternative solution, you will continue to make the same or similar mistakes. Pause for a minute and do some self-work and reflection. What were your family models like growing up? Keep in mind that family models are communication patterns (emotional or verbal) that develop intentionally or unintentionally, consciously or unconsciously, in family systems. As children of those family systems, we learn and adopt these models through observation and experience.

Mirror Neurons

We often learn by watching. The impact of mirror neurons is an important concept to understand. Without getting too technical: Our brains are each made up of approximately eighty-six billion neurons, and these neurons are the infrastructure to our conscious experience.[3] The way God designed us never ceases to amaze me. Yes, our neurons are unique to our own person and experiences, but they can also impact others.

My middle daughter, Elle, is nine years old, and when she was younger, she was a very expressive child and quite demonstrative with her emotions. In one instance, she was so upset that she was having a hard time catching her breath because she was crying so hard. I could have handled her emotions in a few different ways: I could have allowed her crying to affect me and make me upset and then reacted with my own anger or frustration. (This would have made matters worse and escalated things.) I could have ignored her and left her to "deal with" her emotions on her own. Or I could have scooped her up in my arms, sat her on my lap, and held her, making sure I monitored my breathing and my heart rate.

To be completely honest, I've reacted all three ways as a father before, and I'm not proud of the first two since they communicate shame and frustration. As I've grown older and more aware, the third response has become my go-to. Why? Because of the power of mirror neurons. Basically, if I can remain calm, my neurophysiology will emit calmness, and with time and patience, Elle's neurophysiology will begin to mirror mine and move from a state of upset to a state of calm. After enough of these experiences, she will be able to do those same calming strategies on her own because they will be ingrained in her. Unfortunately, this is a two-way street, and if I respond with anger, judgment, or shame, the same neurons will fire in Elle, and she will respond emotionally in kind.

Principle #1: Models matter.

The models we have had deeply impact our current emotional experiences and expression. This is a powerful concept to comprehend, and it can be a difficult one to accept. We don't want to be critical or judgmental of our models, especially if they did the best they could. It can be hard to reflect on our own reactions and the models we are offering to our families and those around us, but it is essential to this conversation. Why do these models matter so much? Models matter because:

1. **They develop expectations.** Expectations can be like formulas. When expectations are developed, they can feel static and immovable, like $2 + 2 = 4$. What we often don't realize is that models are not static but rather malleable, and we can change them with intention. Before we can effectively make the change, we have to recognize what those models are.

2. **They influence our neuropathways.** I love neuroscience. The deeper we dive into the brain, the more clearly we see God. For centuries we believed the brain was unable to change: "What you have is what you get and what you will always have." However, in recent decades we have been able to peel back the complex layers of the brain and recognize the power of models through nurture. Nurture is the way we were raised, and it has a direct influence on how we behave. The reassuring component to this is that even if we had maladaptive models growing up, we have the ability to grow, adapt, and change over time.

3. **They create patterns.** This may seem a bit redundant, but our models create replicable patterns. These patterns do not change until we actually recognize what they are and make the conscious, necessary adjustments.

4. **They can break generational strongholds.** This is my favorite one. When we recognize that models matter and have power, we have the ability to change those models to such a degree that they can break generational strongholds and create a new trajectory for generations to come.

Most often, models are communicated through observation. Unless disrupted, they will continue to be passed down through observation. The motto of one of my college friends was "Be strong. Don't show emotion. Emotion is weakness." I always wondered where that motto came from. One day I asked him.

He sat there for a moment with a puzzled look on his face and said, "I'm not sure."

"Did your mom or dad ever say that to you?" I asked.

"No, I don't think so," he replied. "I only ever remember my dad holding back tears or leaving the room when something became emotional. When his dad died, he didn't even shed a tear, and they were like best friends."

In order for something to change, it must be brought to the surface, it must be brought into the light, and it must be disrupted. If we don't pause and take the necessary time to unpack this idea, the remainder of this book will be pointless. You may be thinking, *Great, Mark! I bought this book to read because I thought it would be a good book for my friend, and now you are asking me to do my own work?!* Yes! Yes, I am! I want you to find relief and freedom when it comes to your emotions. No one gets it right all the time, and no one is perfect. I am still trying to figure things out and am refining my own emotional experiences and expressions. This book, in some ways, is a result of my own journey. These principles are things I try to live out day by day, and my suggestions and reflections are things I've done myself. Don't quickly breeze through these chapters; take some time to slow down and intentionally reflect. Growth is good and growth can be hard; however, without growth we become stagnant, and stagnancy can lead to death (mentally, emotionally, and spiritually). Rise to the challenge and change the trajectory of your life and the lives of generations to come.

Questions for Reflection

1. Who were your main models growing up?

2. How were emotions communicated and expressed by those models?

3. How have those models influenced how you experience, process, and communicate your emotions now?

Action Steps

In the last chapter you were asked to track your most pervasive emotion. Building upon that in your journal, begin to explore where you learned how to express that emotion. Did you learn how to express it by watching and observing? If so, who was involved in those experiences? Is your expression of that emotion beneficial? Do you need to make any changes? If so, what step can you take today?

Note: It takes three cycles of thirty days to make a lasting change. That's how long the brain takes to create new neural pathways. It takes work, patience, and perseverance. Give yourself grace as you embark on this journey. Don't give up!

Part Two

EMOTIONS UNEXPRESSED

3

THE BODY NEVER FORGETS

The mind remembers only certain things.
The body remembers everything.
The information it carries goes back
to the beginning of existence.

JAGGI VASUDEV

Definitions
Cortical limbic system: A set of brain structures including the thalamus, hippocampus, and amygdala that supports a variety of functions, including emotion, behavior, long-term memory, and olfaction (smell).

Frontal lobe: The foremost part of the brain, made up of the left and right frontal cortices, that is responsible for planning appropriate behavioral responses to external and internal stimuli brought on by the cortical limbic system.

Cortisol: A steroid hormone that your adrenal glands and the endocrine glands on the top of your kidneys produce and release. Cortisol mainly regulates your body's stress response.

Trauma: The response to a deeply distressing or disturbing event that overwhelms an individual's ability to cope. It is an internal neurophysiological response to an external stimulus and can cause feelings of helplessness and diminish the sense of self and the ability to feel a full range of emotions.

Trigger: Also known as a stressor, a trigger is an unconscious action or situation that can lead to an adverse emotional response.

I DON'T KNOW ABOUT YOU, but I am amazed by our bodies! We could spend decades exploring the intricacies of just one system. As I contemplated writing this book, I was struck with the notion that we do a good job of creating silos in today's "modern" culture. If we have a sore throat, we go to the medical doctor; if we have a toothache, we go to the dentist; if our back hurts, we go to the chiropractor or physical therapist; and if we are struggling with depression, we go to a therapist. Now, don't get me wrong—each of these specialties is necessary and important, but why do we separate them out? They are all connected and interrelated. My toothache will affect my depression, and my depression will affect my toothache. If this is true, then my unidentified, unacknowledged, or unprocessed emotions are at the root of it all.

Sixth Grade

I tried to focus on the TV screen from across the room, but I couldn't. My eyes wouldn't focus; they were fuzzy and cloudy, with flashes of light emanating from the corners of my eyes. I sighed deeply and thought, *Not again! Why is this happening to me again?* The migraine was back in full force, and without any mercy it threw me into a physical spiral. The blurred vision was just one symptom. My temples were pounding as if someone were using my head as a drum. It seemed like the room was spinning, and I felt like I was going to throw up. I could not find any relief, and this had been going on for several months.

I was in sixth grade, and the migraine headaches seemed to come out of nowhere right after Christmas break. It had been a particularly difficult school year as I struggled to fit in. Two years earlier, we had moved from California to Colorado for my dad's job and to be closer to family. The move was hard on me. California was all I knew, and I had friends there, people who truly got me. I could be my quirky self and be accepted. Colorado was a different story entirely. I knew no one. Maybe you've experienced this very thing and are wondering why it was such a big deal, or maybe you can relate to exactly what I am describing. I was an overly sensitive child and got overwhelmed easily. This was not a good formula for success, for fitting in, or for making friends.

I'm not being completely honest here. Yes, I was a sensitive kid; yes, I was a bit quirky in how I acted and interacted with others; but I also looked like a white version of Steve Urkel from the nineties TV sitcom *Family Matters*. My pants were above my belly button, I had huge glasses, and I had braces. Nineties fashion was unkind to begin with, but it was particularly unkind to me. The kids at my school followed suit and made me the focal point of their ridicule. I was able to blend in during fourth and fifth grades, but something changed in sixth grade. I had a spotlight on me, and I couldn't escape it. I was the main attraction. I would get hip checked into lockers, thrown into trash cans, turned upside down and given swirlies in the toilet. Once, I was locked in a locker, and I'd occasionally be tripped or punched in the back. I have one vivid, traumatic memory of standing up in front of the class and having my pants pulled down by one of the bullies; this time, my underwear came with them. I was mortified but didn't know how to put words to my experiences, so I suffered in silence.

This is when the migraines started. I hadn't yet connected my physical symptoms to my emotional distress, and my parents didn't know what was going on either, so we went the medical route. For months I was tested with blood draws, EEGs, spinal taps, and MRIs, all to see what was causing my pervasive migraines. As you can imagine, they didn't find anything. After my passive suicide attempt,[1] the neurologist pulled my dad aside and suggested we speak with a psychologist because he thought my symptoms did not have a physical root but rather a mental and emotional one. I look back at that pivotal moment and am extremely grateful for that neurologist. My disengaged emotional distress was actively affecting my physiology, and it wasn't good. Once I was able to verbalize and express my emotional backlog, my physiological symptoms began to go away.

Principle #2: Our bodies are always listening and experiencing.

This can be a difficult concept to reconcile. When I say that the body never forgets, I mean that the body is always listening, responding, and storing information. Even when we are asleep, our bodies are taking in information. On one hand, this is slightly disconcerting; on the other, it is amazing. God designed our bodies, our systems, to engage in the world around us consciously and unconsciously.

When we are aware of this, we can use it to our growth and advantage. When we are unaware of this, it can cause damage.

Remember, my definition of *emotions* is "the physiological states brought on by a neurological change associated with thoughts, experiences, and behavioral responses." Something happens to us, and our bodies react. When our bodies react, neurochemicals and hormones are released. When these two things are released, it creates a sensation in our body. We then create thoughts about those experiences and sensations and attempt to give meaning to them based on our language and previous experiences.

From a neurological perspective, sensory information enters the brain through the thalamus. Think of the thalamus as the central processing unit. It takes in information and then distributes it to the proper places. When the thalamus is activated, it also activates the hippocampus and the amygdala. The hippocampus is in charge of familiar memories (*Is this experience familiar? Have I experienced it before? And is it safe?*), whereas the amygdala is the reactive, fight-flight-or-freeze part of the brain. These three components (the thalamus, hippocampus, and amygdala, also known as the cortical limbic system) work in concert with each other to make sure we are kept safe and free from harm.

If that were the only thing that happened in the brain, we would be caught in a perpetual reactionary loop. Instead, we try to make meaning of these physiological experiences. This is done through the anterior cingulate, which connects the cortical limbic system to the frontal lobe of our brain. The frontal lobe is purposefully designed for higher-order thinking. This allows us the opportunity for reason, intellect for planning, and processing. When we are healthy and self-aware, the brain systems allow us to engage in a holistic process of experiencing the world and making meaning from our experiences.

I've not been shy in sharing my own journey with anxiety and depression. I know it is directly linked to my experiences in life, from sixth grade and beyond. My journey has been filled with trial and error, along with intentional practice. I am a more holistic person today because I have an understanding of my struggle, I am aware of my symptoms and triggers, and I can make meaning of the process.

Let me give you an example. We recently made the decision to move. Not from one house to another, but from one state to another. I've lived in Colorado for more than thirty years; it's what I know and what I'm comfortable with. Due to life circumstances and the desire to be closer to family, we decided to move to Texas. I'm excited about the new adventure, but the process of selling and buying a home terrifies me. I like to have things planned out; I like to know what is coming so I can control for variables. Just ask my wife—spontaneity frightens me. So, in the midst of this move, I had to be ready for my emotional reactions. I can't control anything externally but can only control myself internally.

My telltale sign of anxiety surfacing is the inability to catch my breath. My chest gets tight, I feel like there is a twenty-pound weight sitting on me, and I feel like I just ran a marathon. My body is reacting to external stimuli. The cortical limbic system is turned on and is scanning for similar or familiar memories (e.g., sixth grade). When this happens, two distinct pathways open up. The first pathway is that I am caught off guard and I react, staying in the cortical limbic loop of fight, flight, or freeze. This just makes things worse, and I typically end up with a panic attack. The second pathway is that I know my symptoms, I've done the work to connect my cortical limbic system through my anterior cingulate to my frontal lobe, and I make meaning of how my body is feeling. *Oh! I must be stressed, because my chest is tight and I cannot catch my breath. Why is this? This is due to the fact that I cannot see what is coming. Will we sell our home? If so, when? Will we find another home? When will this happen?*

Paying attention to my physical reaction to external stimuli and then starting to make meaning of it begins the process of decompressing my anxiety symptoms. After fifteen or twenty minutes, my chest isn't tight anymore, and my breathing has returned to normal. You might be thinking, *Great! Glad you figured that out, Mark. You have your doctorate in counseling and have helped thousands of people, but that's not me! I feel stuck, and I don't know how to make things any different.* Hang in there with me. Throughout this book I will provide you with practical tools to help you become more holistic in your feeling and thinking.

When We Are Stuck

Remember, the body never forgets. If we haven't learned how to recognize and process our emotions, they stay stuck in our bodies and have the potential to create a mess of problems. When our cortical limbic system is activated and we are unable to make cognitive sense of our experiences, our sympathetic nervous system is also activated, keeping us in a perpetual fight-flight-or-freeze state. In this state, both cortisol and adrenaline are released to keep us in a hyperaroused, alert, and vigilant state. For short periods of time, this is amazing, because it helps us accomplish what we need to in a high-stress, emotional situation. But if the sympathetic nervous system is left on, it can be detrimental to our health.

An activated sympathetic nervous system dilates pupils, inhibits salivation, increases heart rate, opens up airways, and inhibits stomach activity and digestion, preparing you for survival. This keeps us in a heightened awareness state and over time will weaken the immune system, thus creating an open pathway to various diseases. Unresolved emotional experiences can literally make you sick.

Trauma

Trauma complicates being stuck exponentially. When we experience trauma, like I did in sixth grade, our bodies hold on to the physiological sensations and store them away just in case something similar should come along and threaten our safety. The interesting thing about this is that the body is designed to preserve and protect. But unresolved trauma causes significant damage. When we experience trauma, the Broca's area of the brain is inhibited and keeps us from creating language to describe our experience. This is where therapy comes in—we need someone to walk alongside us to begin to make sense of our experiences.

There are two types of trauma. There is major-event trauma, or big-T trauma. This would be something like sexual assault, rape, combat, or a major car accident. This type of traumatic experience is directly linked to a perceived life-or-death situation. When an individual experiences an event like this, his or her entire being goes into survival mode. A heightened sense of awareness is developed, and no person, place, situation, or event is completely safe. The second type of trauma is minor-event trauma, or small-t trauma. This would be something like bullying, emotional manipulation or abuse, shame, or neglect. This type of traumatic experience can be subtle.

Memory

What was your first emotional memory? I know this is an ambiguous question, but I want you to really think about it. I remember mine. I was five or six years old, in kindergarten or first grade. We were living in a small California town, and both my parents were teachers at the same Christian school I attended. One morning, we were rushing to leave. I jumped into the car, and we headed to school. Halfway to school, I realized I still had my fuzzy slippers on. My heart sank, and I began to panic. We were already running late, so I didn't want to say anything to my parents, but for some reason my insecurity spiked. I kept quiet for most of the morning, but during rest time in Mrs. Dubios's class, I lost it and started crying. I can vividly remember crying uncontrollably as the emotional dam broke, releasing fear, insecurity, anxiety, and sadness. I'm amazed at how powerfully I still feel those emotions today, more than thirty years later.

Why do I have the ability to tap into that emotion so vividly? Our brains have the ability to remember significant events. I call them state emotions, and they can be difficult or easy emotions, but they are ingrained and imbedded in us through our experiences. I compare these to state memories. Let me explain.

State memories are our body's reaction to a familiar sensory experience. When I was growing up in California, my grandmother had honeysuckle vines growing on her fence. We would play outside in her backyard for hours on end. Those distinct sensory state memories were embedded into who I am, so much so that when I walk through a candle store and smell something similar to honeysuckle, I am immediately transported back to that memory as if I were actively in her backyard playing. The body is always on, always taking in sensory input and storing it in memories. This can be positive, like my memory of my grandmother's backyard, or it can be difficult, which leads to triggers. Triggers are state memories and emotions that become embedded in our physiology due to traumatic events in our lives. Triggers have a direct effect on our emotional awareness and processing.

So What?

Why does this all matter? It matters because our biological, physiological health is directly related to our emotional health and the expressions therein. We live in a society that is significantly advanced in many ways but seems to be lacking in holistic emotional intelligence. Why? I'm sure there are many factors, but one big reason that comes to mind is our cultural construct of independence. As a society, we create a narrative that we should have it all together, that to express emotion means we are weak. We should instead pull ourselves up by our bootstraps, put on our big-boy or big-girl pants, and get over it. I'm sure you've heard many more such euphemisms, but the bottom line is that many of us have never learned how to express our emotions, and as a result, they are stuck within us and causing physical damage.

I remember a client who came to me for severe depression. Getting to know her over a couple of sessions, it became apparent that she had experienced significant challenges in her life with little to no support. She came to me because I took Medicaid insurance. Her symptoms manifested in typical moderate depression with peripheral physical symptoms of chronic fatigue and intestinal gut issues. As we began to unravel the stories in her life, we were able to create meaning for her by putting language to her experiences. As I watched over the course of several months, I saw her body begin to heal. By putting words and a narrative to her story, we were able to access and name the emotions she experienced. This allowed her body to release the physical side effects of the unexpressed emotions, and she was able to create a more holistic version of herself—mind, body, and spirit.

Questions for Reflection

1. Do you have any unexplained physical symptoms? If so, what are they?

2. Are there parts of your story that you've not been able to put words to?

3. Do you feel like your triggers are right under the surface, ready to pop up without warning?

Action Steps

If you answered yes to any of the questions above, I'd encourage you to consider finding a therapist you can talk with. Why? Because you need someone to help engage in the exploration of these things with you. You cannot do this by yourself, nor should you. Here are three key things to consider when looking for a therapist:

- Create several interview questions to take with you to the initial appointment. Many therapists will provide you with a fifteen- to thirty-minute consultation appointment.

- Give it at least three sessions before you decide to find a different therapist. In my opinion and experience, it can take two to three tries to find the right therapist. It must be someone you can connect with.

- Make sure you are ready to show up. The quality of therapy largely depends on how ready you are for change.

4

HOW ATTACHMENT AFFECTS OUR EMOTIONS

Misbehavior is the expression of an unmet need. If a child needs nurture and I give him structure, I harm his ability to trust me. If a child needs structure and I give him nurture, I harm his ability to grow. Nurture and structure must be used hand in hand.

KARYN PURVIS AND LISA QUALLS,
The Connected Parent: Real Life Strategies for Building Trust and Attachment

Definitions

Reciprocity: "The practice of exchanging things with others for mutual benefit."[1]

Attachment: The development of strong affectional ties between two people through a neurophysiological connection.

Anxious: "Experiencing worry, unease, or nervousness."[2]

Avoidant: "Relating to or denoting a type of personality or behavior characterized by the avoidance of intimacy or social interaction."[3]

Mindset: "The established set of attitudes held by someone."[4]

I'VE COME TO REALIZE THAT LIFE DOESN'T ALWAYS turn out the way we expect. Life can be cruel. It can beat us down, accuse us of things, lie to us, and mislead us. For many, this is the lens through which they see their life. It is one of constant struggle, pain, and disappointment. As I write this, I am confronted with the weight of my comments. They sit like a rock in the pit of my stomach. I also recognize that these thoughts come from the experience of my own life and the hundreds of thousands of stories I have encountered in my fifteen years of counseling. Life is not easy, nor is it fair. It just is.

I remember working with Nathan several years back. Nathan was referred to me by his primary care doctor due to his prolonged and pervasive depression. I will remember my first encounter with Nathan for the rest of my life. He entered my office and sat down on the couch across from my chair. If you are trying to picture this in your mind, let me give you more detail. My couch is a mid-century modern chesterfield in amber leather from Restoration Hardware. Reluctantly, I must admit that it looks very Freudian, something you would see in a Hollywood depiction of a therapist's office. Yes, I bought into that stereotype! Anyway, as Nathan sat on my couch, I realized that something didn't add up. On paper, Nathan was a twenty-nine-year-old successful business professional. In person, he presented as a six-foot-four-inch, 260-pound, quiet, unassuming, and insecure child. I felt the weight of his person even before he set foot in my office. *This guy must have a story,* I thought. *He has to. What I am reading on paper does not line up with what I'm currently experiencing.*

"Nathan," I said, "what brings you in for counseling?"

There was a long, painful pause, then a deep breath. "I'm not able to keep things together at work. I have a hard time with my work relationships."

Listening to Nathan talk, I felt the disorientation of his emotions. I could sense that there was confusion, frustration, sadness, anger, loneliness, and fear. "As you tell me this," I said, "what are you feeling?"

"Feeling? I . . . I don't know," he stammered in frustration.

"Don't worry," I reassured him. "We will figure these things out together."

Nathan and I spent months together unpacking the nuances of his past. He grew up in a strict home. Rules were more important than relationship. He reported that he was often required to complete a task or chore late at night. If things were not a certain way, no one rested until they were. Nathan stated, "I wasn't allowed to cry or show any emotion. If I did, I would be spanked for it. So I kept feelings to myself." He went on to say, "When I was younger, I would cry myself to sleep most nights. Then, as I got older, those tears dried up and turned into anger. I would take my anger out on people at school, on inanimate objects, and sometimes on my pets."

It was evident that Nathan lacked a foundational emotional reciprocity. It wasn't his fault; he hadn't been taught. Furthermore, he experienced a disrupted attachment with his parents. They were not caregivers but rather strict disciplinarians—people of authority, not care. Nathan and I spent many months repairing the damage of his childhood. He worked really hard at destroying the walls that had been built up to keep him from experiencing his emotions. Life had been cruel to him, but he was beginning to see that it didn't have to remain that way.

Principle #3: Our attachments directly affect how we experience and interact with our emotions.

What is attachment, and why is it so important to this conversation? Simply put, *attachment* is the fundamental building block through which our relational and emotional foundations are built. It all starts with the attachment to our primary caregivers, ideally mom and dad. When a baby is born naturally through the birth canal, he receives a dump of oxytocin from mom. Oxytocin, also known as the "cuddle hormone," is released through the umbilical cord as the baby makes his way through the birth canal. This lays the foundation for connection and attachment. If the baby is not born naturally but through a C-section, the oxytocin dump can happen through skin-on-skin contact with both his mom and his dad. If the baby is born and struggles with health issues or is premature, this has the potential to disrupt the initial attachment imprinting and can cause mental and emotional issues later in life. Remember, if attachment is created between parent and child, it has the potential to be recreated when it gets disrupted. This is where we find hope in this conversation as God provides a way for healing and redemption through relationship.

I had a premature birth. At my recent fortieth birthday celebration, my dad brought pictures of me as a newborn. My girls loved seeing these pictures. I was tiny—four pounds nine ounces at birth and almost two months early. My dad shared with my girls that the small California town where we lived could not accommodate a premature birth, so my parents and their friends drove sixty miles to Community Memorial Hospital in Ventura, California.

My mom jokes that I could have very easily been born in the car. My dad said, "I was told that if he made it through the night, he would be okay." I survived the night and then spent several weeks in an incubator hooked up to a breathing tube and heart monitor. My parents could be by my side, but they could only interact with me through the machine. Yes, I survived, but I missed out on some of the fundamental building blocks I mentioned.

The deficits didn't resurface until I was in early grade school, and they showed up in the form of separation anxiety. Separation anxiety is an attachment disruption where a child becomes excessively anxious when separated from parents. Separation anxiety can often go unnoticed or be mislabeled as "clinginess." It is often triggered by stress and leaves the child preoccupied with irrational thoughts and fears, unable to think about anything else but the present fear of separation. These fears and anxieties can be manifested in nightmares and often keep the child from going to school or other places.

I vividly remember my first experience with separation anxiety. I was invited over to my neighborhood friend Christopher's house for a sleepover. Our moms were close, and we saw each other often. We lived only a couple of blocks apart. Up until this time, all our playdates had been during the day. This would be the first overnight. The day leading up to the sleepover was an exciting one. I daydreamed about the adventures we would have. The time came to go over to Christopher's home. My bags were packed, and I was ready! As my dad was driving me over, I got a twinge of anxiety in my stomach. I ignored it. That afternoon was a blast! Everything went according to plan until it was time for bed. The twinge of anxiety I had ignored hours earlier was beginning to creep up into a full-fledged panic. My mind started racing, my palms became sweaty, and I could not stop shaking. I started to cry (insert shame here) and frantically asked Christopher's parents to call my dad to come pick me up. I was mortified that I had disappointed my friend, but I could not be away from my parents. My dad came and picked me up. I don't remember what was said on the car ride home or if I was able to express what I was feeling, but I do remember the immediate relief of crawling into my bed when I got home.

Types of Attachment

It wasn't until I was in my master's program that I realized I struggled with separation anxiety and that it was directly related to my birth trauma. Before I discuss the direct correlation between attachment and emotions, let me first break down the different attachment styles.

Secure Attachment

A secure attachment is the ideal form of attachment. This means that the attachment to our primary caregivers was healthy and intact. The necessary building blocks were laid, and a clear sense of identity and purpose was developed. I personally like how psychiatrist Daniel Siegel talks about a secure attachment in his book *Brainstorm*. He states that there are three key components to a secure attachment: being seen, feeling safe, and feeling soothed.

1. **Being seen.** This means that our inner mental and emotional life is sensed beneath the outward behavior. Our caregiver hears our cry, figures out what our inner need is, and then offers us something to meet that need.

2. **Feeling safe.** This means that we are both protected from harm (mentally, emotionally, physically, and spiritually) and not terrified by our caregiver.

3. **Feeling soothed.** This means that when we are distressed, our caregiver's response makes us feel better.[5]

Therefore, according to Siegel, a secure attachment serves as a launching pad from which we can take off to explore the world around us. When we have a secure-attachment model, we have the security to venture out into all that lies in the world.

Let me illustrate this with a story. When Hannah, my oldest, was young, she loved to play on the playground next to our townhome complex. Before her siblings were born, we lived in a gated townhome community. We didn't have a backyard, but there was a magnificent park at the end of our cul-de-sac that we often frequented. I would sit on the park bench and allow Hannah to venture off and explore the playground.

There were many things she would do on her own, and some things she would need my help with. I remember one day she wanted to climb the rock wall. I went up to help her and she said, "No, Daddy! I got it!" So I stepped back and allowed her to try. On her first attempt she managed to make it halfway up (about three feet off the ground) and then fell, scraping her knee. Crying, she got up and came over to me. I scooped her up and held her as she cried. I told her how proud I was of her and how brave she was for trying. Several minutes of holding her passed, and she calmed down. After several more minutes passed, she climbed down off my lap and went back to playing. I'd seen her and her struggle, I'd become a safe place for her, and I'd soothed her. Because of that security, she was now able to venture out and try again.

Insecure Attachment

I wish that all attachments were secure attachments, but in a fallen world this isn't the case. There are two types of insecure attachment styles I'd like to discuss and illustrate.

ANXIOUS ATTACHMENT

The first type of insecure attachment is anxious attachment. I'm sure you have already determined in your mind what this would look like, since its root is anxiety. An anxious attachment is rooted in control. What do I mean by "control"? Simply put, such an individual must have control over various aspects of their life. When they feel out of control, their anxiety is triggered, and they'll do anything or everything they can to regain that control. This is often manifested in relationships. When someone with anxious attachment is in a relationship, they find safety in micromanaging their significant other. Vulnerability is an unknown variable and as such creates anxiety; with that anxiety comes control, and with control come manipulation and walls. The goal is to control and to protect.

How does an anxious attachment form? Unlike the stable base of a secure attachment, the child with an anxious attachment is often either left to figure things out on their own or is micromanaged by a "helicopter" parent. Essentially, there is uncertainty about how the parent will react or respond, which pushes the child into a state of dysregulation and anxiety.

Going back to the example of my oldest, Hannah, at the playground, let's say the same scenario of the rock wall happened, but this time I was a helicopter parent and followed her around the playground. Instead of letting her try new things, I would hover to make sure she didn't get hurt. I would obsess about her safety; my anxiousness would spill over onto her.

But let's take it a step further. Let's say I turn my back for a second and she attempts to climb that rock wall. As I turn back around, I see her fall. Instead of picking her up and holding her as she cries, I berate her for not listening to me and chastise her for her mistake. Those mixed messages compound the disrupted attachment, and she creates a narrative: *Daddy cares about me, but he's mad at me when I get hurt. Therefore, I must be hypervigilant too.*

Then let's say the next time we go to the park I am aloof in how I engage with Hannah. She's left to play however she wants, and when she falls this time, I don't react at all. My inconsistency as a parent is now creating fear, anxiety, and uncertainty in Hannah. If I continue to parent in this way, an anxious attachment style will develop in her, making it difficult for her to maneuver in this world.

AVOIDANT ATTACHMENT

The second type of insecure attachment is avoidant attachment. Again, the type of attachment response can be ascertained in the wording. Avoidant attachment style is indicative of putting people at arm's length, not allowing people to get close. Individuals with an avoidant attachment struggle to get close to those around them and/or maintain healthy relationships at all. Often those with an avoidant attachment style are described as having a huge wall around them; they only let people get so close.

Using the same scenario with Hannah and the playground, let's say she's playing and I'm sitting on the bench, and she is trying everything she can to get me to notice, but I am preoccupied and on my phone. She attempts to climb the rock wall and falls, scraping her knee. She cries out for help, but I remain disconnected and aloof. After some time, she finds a way to self-soothe. If this pattern became consistent, she would create the internal narrative

I have to care for myself because no one else will. She would then develop a deep mistrust of people. However, this would come in direct conflict with how God created us, and now she would be caught in the middle: *Life has taught me to take care of myself; no one can be trusted. Yet I have such a deep desire to be seen, valued, and loved that I attempt relationships, but when they get too close, something is triggered in me and I avoid depth at all costs.* Now she'd be stuck in this maladaptive relational cycle.

Attachment and Our Emotions

I've provided you with a very basic overview of attachment. Countless individuals have devoted their lives to the study of attachment and its impact on our mental, emotional, physical, and spiritual functioning. Here is what I would like for you to take away from this conversation:

- **Your attachment experiences matter.** You should not gloss over your early experiences. They have a direct impact on your mental, emotional, physical, and spiritual functioning today.

- **Your attachment experiences lay a foundation for your emotional lens.** Has someone ever told you that you have rose-colored glasses on? Or that you see the world as a glass half empty or half full? These expressions describe the lens through which you see the world. Your attachment experiences shape that. I want you to hear me say this: Your experiences matter, *and* they should not be viewed as absolute truth. What do I mean by that? If you had a bad experience with your father, you may think that all men are not trustworthy. You take your subjective experience and extrapolate it to the whole. This can be a dangerous path because it has the potential to keep you stuck. Each of us must find ways to value and validate our subjective experiences while simultaneously striving to explore objective alternatives.

- **Your attachment experiences don't have to dictate your future.** The beautiful thing about human beings created in the image of the triune God is that we have the ability to grow and change over time. With a changed mindset (moving from fixed to growth), you can work toward altering your view of yourself from a victim of your circumstances to a survivor or thriver.

Yes, our relational attachment stories matter. We must talk about them, understand them, and explore the meaning within them. However, they are not static or immovable; they should inform us of our past, create understanding for our present, and propel us to make different, more informed decisions about our future. The deeper we go, the richer our story becomes.

Questions for Reflection

1. Have you ever reflected on your attachment story? If so, what have you discovered?

2. What were your relational models growing up?

3. How have your relational models impacted your current functioning?

4. Would you say you have a primarily secure attachment, anxious attachment, or avoidant attachment?

Action Steps

Exploring your attachment story can be somewhat overwhelming. Take it step by step; don't try to explore it all at once. The best thing you can do is to bracket it; this means allotting fifteen minutes a day to explore your attachment story. Set a timer. Once the timer goes off, put your pen down and close your journal. Pick it back up tomorrow. It would also be good to walk through this process with someone else. If you don't have a therapist (as discussed last chapter), do you have a significant other or friend you can process with?

5

AVOIDANCE IS NEVER THE ANSWER

With the avoidance of pain,
we lose the healing, too.

UNKNOWN

Avoidance doesn't solve anything;
it merely serves as a temporary salve.
TONY DUNGY, *Uncommon:*
Finding Your Path to Significance

Definitions

Pain: "[Mental, emotional, and/or] physical suffering or discomfort caused by illness or injury."[1]

Avoidance: "The action of keeping away from or not doing something"; "the action of preventing something from happening."[2]

Reflex: "An action that is performed as a response to a stimulus and without conscious thought"; "an automatic response to a stimulus."[3]

I DON'T KNOW ABOUT YOU, but I'm not a big fan of pain. In fact, I try to avoid it as often as I possibly can. One of my least favorite places to go is the dentist. Every time I go, I experience some form of discomfort or pain. My mouth is a sensitive place, and when they are in there with their picks, their needles, and their drills, it hurts. So I try hard to avoid going to the dentist. So does my wife, Sarah, for the same reason.

But one Christmas, we had an emergency. Sarah had been complaining about a sore shoulder. Thinking she had slept on it wrong, she went to a chiropractor and was able to find some relief. But over the next couple of days, the pain got worse. Then one night she woke me up in excruciating pain. This scared me, because Sarah has a pretty high pain tolerance, so if *she* is in excruciating pain, it is a big deal. I rushed her to the emergency room, and after a couple of tests they concluded it was an impacted and abscessed tooth. The pain she was experiencing was referral pain from the nerve root to that tooth.

Over the course of four weeks, she went back and forth to the dentist to have a series of root canals. The process was one she does not want to repeat. As I was thinking about these events, I wondered, *Could they have been avoided?* Maybe a consistent appointment at the dentist would have caught the early stages of tooth decay. What it taught me is that a little pain or discomfort every six months could prevent the possibility of immense pain later.

Avoidance

What does it mean to avoid? Is avoidance a conscious action or a subconscious protective mechanism? A basic definition of *avoidance* is "the action of keeping away from or not doing something" or "the action of preventing something from happening." The question then becomes *What are we keeping away from or preventing from happening?* For many of us, the answer is emotional pain or the perception of emotional pain.

Pain is defined as "physical suffering or discomfort caused by illness or injury" or "mental suffering or distress." Though this is a straightforward definition, it doesn't give us the bigger picture. Why as human beings do we naturally avoid pain? How is pain manifested in our physiology?

Physical Manifestation of Pain

How does pain work in the body? Let's say you put your hand on a hot stove. Here is what happens to the body:

- Tissue is damaged, and it awakens microscopic pain receptors called nociceptors in your skin. Each receptor forms one end of a nerve cell. On the other end are the spinal cord and central nervous system. When a pain receptor is activated, it sends electrical signals up the nerve fiber.

- Once the nerve fiber is activated, it bonds with a bunch of other nerves and sends the signals up the spinal cord to the neck.

- In the base of the neck is an area called the dorsal horn, where the signals are transmitted from one nerve cell to the next and passed from the spinal cord to the brain.

- Once in the brain, the signals are passed to the thalamus, which then sends them to the proper areas of the brain. In this case the signals are sent to the somatosensory cortex (responsible for physical sensations), the frontal cortex (in charge of thinking and reasoning), and the limbic system (linked to emotional reaction).

The end result is that you "feel" pain, think or say *Ouch*, and then react accordingly. The interesting thing is that this happens so quickly that you most likely react involuntarily or subconsciously even before you are aware of the situation. It is a reflex reaction. This is virtually the same process our body goes through with emotions, which create an emotional reflex.

Principle #4: Emotional avoidance will hinder our ability to process feelings and, after time, will only give way to anger.

The Emotional-Pain Reflex

If you think about it, the same reflex response happens to us emotionally as well. When was the last time you experienced a difficult or painful emotion? What was your reflex? (Remember, a reflex is "an action that is performed as a response to a stimulus and without conscious thought" or "an automatic response to a stimulus.")

Leah had been a regular client for almost thirty sessions. She was in her late twenties and college educated, and she came from an upper-middle-class family. She worked for a successful tech company and made six figures. From the outside looking in, one would surmise that Leah had it all together. We had been working on some significant life transitions, and she seemed to be making progress, but I always felt like I was missing something. I didn't think she was being dishonest with me, but something didn't add up.

Her presenting problem was that she needed help working through her divorce of almost a year earlier and her desire to remarry one day without making the same mistakes. She disclosed that she and her ex-husband had met during their freshman year of college and gotten married less than a year later. As we began to peel back the layers, it became evident that they had jumped into the relationship without much thought. They did not have good relational models or boundary models, and as a result, their marriage was doomed from the start. In therapy we were able to create and develop the missing foundation and craft what she wanted her future to look like, but still, there was something else that was not being discussed in therapy, and I could not put my finger on it. So, after thirty sessions, I was prepared to graduate her from therapy. The day came for our termination session, and I could tell something was off.

"Leah," I said, "I'm noticing your demeanor is different today than it normally is. What is going on?"

"Umm . . . I . . . uh," she stammered. "I've not been completely honest with you." She looked away from me. In a gentle voice I asked, "What do you mean?" She looked up and caught my gaze and then quickly looked away again. "I haven't shared with you the real reason for my divorce."

By this time, I could feel the tension in the room. I immediately thought, *The real reason?! What have we been working on the past six months?* I kept my cool and didn't let on to my surprise.

"Leah, it's okay. Tell me more." That was the invitation she needed. She spent the next forty-five minutes dumping everything she had kept from me. It turns out Leah had been struggling with pornography, and coupled with the marital struggles, that became the final straw in their marriage.

We spent the next couple of months unpacking this new revelation and concluded that pornography had become Leah's reflex to difficult and painful emotions. Once we were able to determine this, I was able to help her become more emotionally present and whole, and she was able to move forward in life with a holistic perspective on her emotional experiences.

Here is what I want you to focus on: A reflex only stays a reflex if we don't put thought and action into it. An emotional reflex becomes our instant reaction to internal or external stimuli. It is just like our leg spastically kicking when the doctor hits our knee: Our emotional reflexes can be all over the place. It is important to take a step back and begin to assess what your emotional reflexes are. Sometimes it helps to have an outside perspective to provide insight into this conversation. I would encourage you to draw in a safe person to be a sounding board in this process.

Five Ways We Avoid Our Emotions

Can you relate to Leah? I know I sure can. When we develop an avoidance reflex, it can become difficult for it to change. This is why it is so important that we have people in our lives who can help us make sense of these things. Here are five ways I believe we avoid difficult or painful emotions:

1. **We numb.** One of the most effective ways to avoid something difficult or painful is to numb. I may step on some toes here, but I want you to stick with me. Some of the most common ways to numb are through things like addiction to alcohol or other substances, overeating, and pornography.

When we choose to numb, we create a dopamine dump in our brains that allows us to escape discomfort and feel good for the time being. The dopamine dump creates an effective escape from the realities of life, but over time, the feel-good dopamine dump becomes a numbing reflex that can take on a detrimental, addictive quality. The more we use this response, the more we need it to cope.

2. **We distract.** Distraction is an effective strategy because it shifts our focus from the difficult or painful to something more palatable. One of my biggest forms of distraction is television. When I am struggling, I find it easy to get lost in a movie or binge-watch a television show. Another good distraction is the plethora of games on our smartphones. If we are struggling, it's easy and enticing to distract ourselves with Solitaire, Wordle, or Candy Crush. For a brief moment we forget that we are struggling with a difficult or painful emotion. In the short term, a distraction like this is okay; however, if this is our long-term coping strategy, the difficult or painful emotions will continue to build and often become more intense once the distraction is over.

3. **We stay busy.** I will say, this is what I struggle with most. If I stay busy, if I stay focused on something external, if I work toward a goal, a new adventure, or a new dream, I don't have to sit with or acknowledge my difficult or painful emotions. For me, being busy is very effective, albeit unhealthy.

4. **We replace it.** This could seem very similar to numbing, and in some ways it is. However, I look at this as slightly different. In my mind and experience, replacing

can look like overexercising, oversleeping, diving headfirst into a hobby or adrenaline-seeking behavior, and so on. We can also replace dealing with a difficult or painful emotion by being hyperspiritual or hyperoptimistic. In some ways this idea of replacing allows us to ignore what is truly going on.

5. **We overindulge in self-help.** This one is tricky. Why? Because for all intents and purposes, self-help is a good thing. Right? Yes . . . and it can do a couple of things that are not beneficial. First, it can overfill our heads with knowledge and make us lose the ability to connect that knowledge to practice. I'm sure you've met someone who has possessed immense knowledge but lacked the willingness, desire, or awareness to apply it to her own life. Second, overindulgence in self-help can puff us up with pride. We think we know it all, so it applies to everyone else but us, and we are quick to judge.

I'm sure there are many more ways we can avoid our difficult or painful emotions, but these are the most common ones I've seen or experienced myself.

Reasons We Avoid

The reasons we avoid difficult or painful emotions are complex. Going back to what I mentioned about my distaste for the dentist, I can easily say that I avoid the dentist because of a previous bad experience, because of fear, because of misinformation, because of stigma, and because I am uneducated about the benefits. I think these are also some of the same reasons we avoid difficult or painful emotions. Let's unpack these reasons further.

1. **A previous bad experience.** If you've had a bad experience, are you excited and willing to try the same thing again? The answer is probably no. Experience is often the most effective teacher, whether right or wrong. I remember being an overly emotional kid growing up. I would often react with strong emotions and/or break down into tears. The typical response of my parents was to send me to my room to "calm down." Hindsight tells me that this was their way of giving me space to process. In the moment, though, what it taught me was that my emotions were bad and not welcome in our home. Now I realize that that was an extreme interpretation, and as I've talked with my parents, I've learned that it wasn't at all their intention. However, this was the meaning I made from my experience, and it was not helpful. My interpretation of my emotional experience led me to bottle up my difficult and painful emotions, which eventually led to my suicide attempt in sixth grade.

2. **Fear.** I love the song "Fear Is a Liar" by Zach Williams. This is a true statement, but in the moment, fear can be pretty convincing when it comes to our emotional experiences:

   - *Don't do it! It'll only make it worse.*
   - *This is what you deserve.*
   - *Don't even bother; your painful emotions will never go away.*
   - *You are so stupid! Why would you think it could be any different?*

Fear creates a narrative that keeps us stuck. We convince ourselves that the pain of the present is less painful than the pain of processing or confronting the emotions, and we stay stuck.

3. **Misinformation.** Growing up in church I often heard Jeremiah 17:9 quoted when it came to emotions: "The heart is deceitful above all things, and desperately sick; who can understand it?" (ESV). At face value, this verse looks as if it is saying that the heart and emotions are deceitful and bad and shouldn't be trusted. As a child, no one gave me any other context for this verse, nor was there any further explanation. So in my mind, my emotions were bad. It wasn't until I was much older that I read the verse in context. It says, "The heart is hopelessly dark and deceitful, a puzzle that no one can figure out. But I, GOD, search the heart and examine the mind. I get to the heart of the human. I get to the root of things. I treat them as they really are, not as they pretend to be" (Jeremiah 17:9-10). Wow! What a difference context makes. It is not saying to ignore or avoid our emotions; it is saying that due to the sinful condition of our hearts they may not always tell the truth, but we should pay attention to what they are saying and take them to God or a trustworthy friend for deeper investigation.

4. **Stigma.** I am not a big fan of stigma. *Stigma* is defined as "a mark of disgrace associated with a particular circumstance, quality, or person."[4] We have stigmatized a lot of things in our society—emotions, mental illness, and pain, to name a few. Because of its stigma, many of us create a skewed narrative and avoid emotion at all costs, just like I did with the dentist. The false narrative is convincing, and it must be confronted in a way that replaces the stigma with the truth.

5. **Being uneducated about the benefits.** Where do you get your information? In the "free-market information age," we can pretty much find something on the Internet to support whatever our narrative might be, even if it is false. As I was preparing to write this book, I searched "Are emotions good or bad?" on Google and found competing information. Before Google, where did we go to find reliable information? We would seek out the truth in people's experiences and take the time to ask the experts. Frankly, nothing has changed. If you want something to be different, you need to put in the work to make it different. In this case, the pain of pushing through your emotions is and will be less than the pain of remaining where you are.

Remember, this is not the time to bring shame or guilt into this conversation. We *all* have avoidance behaviors, and we *all* have specific emotional reflexes. Listening to the lies of shame and/or guilt will only make matters worse. This is an opportunity to push off the lie that you are "less than" or "defective" and take intentional steps toward growth and healing.

Questions for Reflection

1. What has been your experience with mental and emotional pain?

2. Have you ever reflected on your avoidance behaviors? If so, what have you noticed to be your typical reaction? If not, what has kept you from this reflection?

3. What is your typical emotional reflex?

Action Steps

Take some time this week to observe your emotional reflexes. Don't judge them; just observe and report. The only way we can effectively make changes is to know what we are actually dealing with.

THE IMPORTANCE
OF FORGIVENESS

*Forgiveness, I believe, is a virtue. And a virtue classically is
something that is a positive character trait, a positive character
strength that people have, in which they do something that's good.
In positive psychology, we look at this nowadays as what is
called a* eudaimonic *virtue, and that's just a Greek term that
means it's good for ourselves, but it is also good for other people.
It just kind of takes that traditional Greek* eudaimonia *and shifts
it a little bit, but it's a . . . goodness of character, a character strength
that not only is good for me but is also good for other people.*

EVERETT L. WORTHINGTON JR.[1]

Definitions
Forgive(ness): "To stop feeling angry or resentful toward
someone for an offense, flaw, or mistake; to cancel debt."[2]

Trespass: "[To] make unfair claims on or take advantage of
([someone or] something)"; "[to] commit an offense against
(a person or a set of rules)."[3]

Humble: "Having or showing a modest or low estimate of one's
own importance"; "of modest pretensions or dimensions."[4]

Empathy: "The ability to understand and share the feelings of another."[5]

Shame: "A painful feeling of humiliation or distress caused by the consciousness of wrong or foolish behavior; a regrettable or unfortunate situation or action."[6]

HAVE YOU EVER BEEN WRONGED by someone? I know that's a pretty ridiculous question; of course you have, and so have I. How did you respond? Did you forgive them immediately and move on? Did you let it affect you for a while? Or did you work through the nuances of the situation, allow yourself to feel, and then make the choice to forgive? Emotions and forgiveness go hand in hand, and they affect us more than you might think.

Several years ago I experienced something very difficult. I founded and ran a rather large counseling nonprofit. We had around thirty staff members and served tens of thousands of clients per year. It was 2020, and we were doing everything we could to survive during the pandemic. Leading during that time was very difficult, and to make matters worse, I almost lost my dad to a botched cancer surgery around the same time. I had been doing my best to find creative ways to keep the company afloat. We took out a government-assistance loan made available to us, found several grants, and kept seeing clients virtually, but it wasn't enough to keep the doors open. So we had to make a decision. We had to cut pay.

I know, I know—you don't mess with people's pay, and I wish we hadn't had to, but the alternative was to lay everyone off and close our doors. After several months of wrestling with the board of directors, we finally made the decision to reduce pay. Some people received a $250-per-month pay cut, while others received a $1,000-per-month pay cut. These decisions were made based on each person's longevity at the company, education, and licensure status. During this process, I lost sleep, my anxiety and depression spiked, and I lost my appetite, among other things. It was hard.

The day came to make the announcement, which had to be done over Zoom due to the ongoing pandemic. In full transparency, I wish I had met with each staff member individually, because the rollout of the changes was a disaster. I wasn't expecting it to be easy, but I was expecting some understanding based on the circumstances of the past year. I was given that courtesy from some, but the majority of the staff reacted out of emotion. Many things were said disparaging my leadership, both to my face and behind my back. Over the course of the next three months, about a dozen staff members chose to quit.

I was deeply hurt by the circumstances and by the way people chose to leave. It was a very difficult season in my life. (I'm positive all who left would say the same thing, but from a different perspective.) My pride was hurt. I wanted to defend myself, to react, but I couldn't. Instead, I held on to the offenses and internalized them as a leader. Instead of processing the offenses, forgiving them, and moving on, I felt justified in holding a grudge and allowed myself to become bitter. As "emotionally intelligent" as I thought I was, I let myself become defensive and defiant, and it consumed me for quite some time. I knew it wasn't healthy, but in the moment I didn't care.

Things didn't change much for me until about eight months later. I was reading the book *Psychology, Theology, and Spirituality in Christian Counseling* by Mark McMinn. In it he discusses the idea that forgiveness is the choice to wrestle with either an internal or an external offense so we can process through the emotional landscape and come out stronger on the other side.[7] That statement hit me like a ton of bricks. I was making the choice to stay stuck. I was allowing the imprint of what had happened to keep me imprisoned in bitterness. I needed to find a way to stop identifying with the trespass and find freedom from it. But how? I had to allow myself to sit with the tension of what was happening, to feel all my feelings and work through the stages of the emotional process. (Note: This is different from the process of lament, which we will explore more in the next chapter.)

Principle #5: Harboring unforgiveness is death to our emotions and eventually our souls.

Stages of Emotional Process

If principle #5 is true, and I believe it is, how do we begin to process our unforgiveness and allow our emotions to heal? Here are several steps that I've used in my own healing journey and find very helpful:

1. **Acknowledge the pain.** Why would I want to acknowledge the pain? Isn't the goal to not feel it? If I acknowledge the pain, then it confirms it's there, right? I hate to break it to you, but the pain of a trespass is there whether you acknowledge it or not. By acknowledging the pain, you begin to provide language and context to the trespass.

   Example: I was deeply hurt by people's words, actions, and reactions. It hurt my feelings, I felt betrayed, sad, and disappointed, and it was a blow to my pride.

2. **Grieve it.** When I say "grieve it," some people think I'm talking about the stages of grief. I am not; in fact, Elisabeth Kübler-Ross's stages of grief were designed to help those with terminal illnesses process their mortality, which is very different from what I'm referring to here. What I mean is allowing yourself to experience the loss. To do this, you need to engage in your awareness around both the emotion (how your body is responding) and the feeling (the context through which you process the emotion based on your cultural understanding of that emotion). In our Western culture, we far too often desire to "get over" the experience versus "move through" the experience. The following diagram gives a visual of how I conceptualize the grieving process.

Example: Instead of fighting the feelings I had, I allowed them to come. I followed the aspects of the Grief Diagram and went through the process. It wasn't as smooth as it looks in the diagram, but it created space for me to process without judgment.

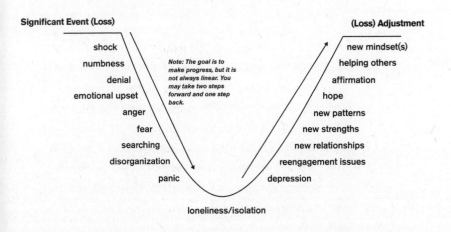

Significant Event (Loss)

shock
numbness
denial
emotional upset
anger
fear
searching
disorganization
panic

Note: The goal is to make progress, but it is not always linear. You may take two steps forward and one step back.

loneliness/isolation

(Loss) Adjustment

new mindset(s)
helping others
affirmation
hope
new patterns
new strengths
new relationships
reengagement issues
depression

3. **Humility.** This was a hard one. Humility demands that we take a step back and own our own mistakes regarding a trespass. Holding unforgiveness in our hearts causes us to point fingers to anything external, whereas humility requires us to look inward.

    Example: I had to own the fact that I did not handle the rollout of the changes well, and I had to recognize that the way I led during that time created deeper issues.

4. **Empathy.** In the process of forgiveness, we must attempt to put ourselves in the other person's shoes. This is a big task—our human nature wants to cling to our justification and hold a grudge. Empathy helps us put down the defenses and experience what someone else is experiencing.

    Example: I must admit, this was a difficult one for me. I was so caught up in my reasons for making the decision and justifying my actions that when I stopped to put myself in my staff's shoes, I realized that they, too, had been through a rough year and the pay cut added insult to injury.

5. **Release.** This step is an ongoing process, but this is where you release the offense. My favorite prayer for this step is *Lord, I give everyone and everything to you.* It doesn't "fix" much, but it is an intentional mental decision to release the offense to God.

    Example: When I would get worked up over the situation, I would verbally pray that prayer out loud, then journal about the specifics of what was bothering me, and then verbally read aloud the content of my journal. There is something about reading something aloud that makes it real. You hear it differently.

6. **Accept.** This step is a mental process whereby you recognize what actually happened and accept that this is now a part of your story. You cannot change it; it has happened, and now the effects of what has transpired are a permanent part of your story.

   Example: I had to accept that I lost friends over this. I had to accept their responses, whether or not they sought restoration. I had to accept the new normal.

7. **Integrate.** The final step is to integrate the experience into your life and remember the impact it had, learn from it, and move forward. This step also requires you to lay down any lingering emotions you've been holding on to.

   Example: I truly learned from this experience. I learned how to be a better leader and how to make better boundaries, and I learned to sit with and process my intense feelings about being hurt and betrayed. As a result, I am a much stronger person.

In complete transparency, this is still a process for me. When emotions come back up, I have to recognize what they are and where they are coming from, and I intentionally work through the seven steps again. One of the individuals who left chose to reach out again, wanting to meet and reconnect. I had to evaluate the situation and make a decision based on this process. I ended up choosing not to reconnect. It wasn't because I had ill feelings toward that individual; it was because they had no reciprocal understanding or awareness of how their actions had affected me and my family. I chose to put up a boundary. Yes, I have forgiven them, but it doesn't mean they get full access to me or my family. Remember, forgiveness is not a "one and done" progression; it is a continuous, intentional mindset in which we actively step into the process of being freed from being identified with the trespass.

The Roadblock of Shame

I don't know about you, but I find it easier to forgive others than to forgive myself. I am my worst critic and at times my own worst enemy. Can you relate? Shame has a way of grabbing a megaphone and screaming negativity and lies into our minds. If we do not confront these disruptive narratives, they can become commonplace and derail our journey toward emotional healing and freedom.

I had been working with Abby for almost six weeks. Abby struggled with confidence in all aspects of her life. She struggled in her work as a teacher, she struggled in her relationships, and she struggled in her faith. She was an attractive, petite thirty-two-year-old who grew up in a very conservative Christian household. Though she dressed stylishly, she wore clothes that were two sizes too big. She wore minimal makeup, and her hair was six inches past her shoulders. Initially she struggled to maintain eye contact with me, and she spoke in such muted tones that I often had to ask her to repeat herself because I could not hear her.

Today was our sixth session. In the past five sessions, we had talked about "surface-y" stuff, but I could tell she was holding something back. After some time reflecting and praying prior to the session, I felt it was time to confront this feeling I had.

"Abby," I said, "I've enjoyed working with you these past several weeks. I've reflected on our time together, and I'm confronted with the realization that you've not been fully honest with me."

I paused. I could tell I had hit a nerve. Abby began shifting in her seat and looking around the room. I waited and patiently held the space for her to process whether or not she was going to say anything. After several minutes, she looked up with tears streaming down her face and said, "I'm so ashamed! If I tell you, you are going to think differently of me."

I calmly reassured her that there was nothing she could say that would affect my view of her and that this counseling relationship was a safe and confidential space for her to process her struggles. Upon hearing that, she took a deep breath and proceeded to tell me this story.

"I was sixteen years old," she began. "I was young and naive. I was dating a boy from my youth group. My parents didn't know, because if they had, I would not have been allowed to date him. During our church's summer camp, one night I snuck out of the girls dorm to meet up with him. One thing led to another and we ended up sleeping together." She paused and her lower lip began to quiver. "L-l-less than a month later, I found out I was pregnant. I was mortified. I couldn't tell my parents, so I kept it a secret as long as I could. But after about four months, I couldn't make up any more excuses and they found out."

Abby stopped, took a big, deep breath, and continued. "Their reaction was worse than I could have imagined. They lost it. They berated me, called me names, yelled, cried, and then were silent. From the moment they found out, I lost any choice or control I had. They started making decisions for me, sent me to my aunt's house to finish out the pregnancy, and then decided to give the baby up for adoption without my consent. Six months later, I came home as if nothing had ever happened, and we haven't talked about it since."

We spent the next several sessions continuing to process the story. We utilized narrative therapy to help her tell the story in as much detail as possible. The hope was to help give her back control of the narrative and find ways to tell her story in full. We then spent a great deal of time slowly going through the process outlined above (acknowledge the pain, grieve it, etc.). The hardest part for Abby was rewriting the shame narrative. Her shame had become a familiar character in her story, and it needed to be confronted. Once we were able to tease out the actual narrative, we could begin replacing it with the truths of who she really was. I'm not sure what happened to Abby; it has been more than ten years since our last appointment. I hope she was able to apply the work we did together into a lasting narrative of hope, joy, and forgiveness. I hope she was able to reconnect with her daughter, which was one of her therapeutic goals.

A note of importance from Abby's story: Shame is powerful, and it has the potential to disrupt and/or derail our mental and emotional health. Shame quietly whispers, *You messed up. Who do you think you are? You are a failure, you are worthless, and you won't amount to anything, so don't even bother* and many similar narratives. Shame will keep you stuck in your mental and emotional spiral until you drag it into the light of truth. We cannot do this on our own; we need others to help us with this process. Once shame is brought into the light, it cannot survive.

Questions for Reflection

1. Is there any unresolved unforgiveness in your life?

2. If so, how is this unforgiveness affecting you?

3. Is there any shame that is holding on from a past decision? What steps do you need to take to forgive yourself?

Action Steps

This is your week! If you have any lingering unforgiveness, I want you to write out the trespass in its entirety. Do not spare any detail. Then I want you to work your way through the seven steps of emotional process. Remember, forgiveness is a process—do not rush through it.

Part Three

EMOTIONS
EXPRESSED

7

PAY ATTENTION
TO THE TENSION

Maturity is achieved when a person accepts life as full of tension.

JOSHUA LOTH LIEBMAN,
Peace of Mind

Definitions

Tension: "The state of being stretched tight"; "a relationship between ideas or qualities with conflicting demands or implications."[1]

Friend: "A person whom one knows and with whom one has a bond of mutual affection"; "a person who acts as a supporter of a cause"; "a person who is not an enemy or who is on the same side."[2]

Perseverance: "Persistence in doing something despite difficulty or delay in achieving success."[3]

Patience: "The capacity to accept or tolerate delay, trouble, or suffering without getting angry or upset."[4]

Practice: "The actual application or use of an idea, belief, or method, as opposed to theories relating to it."[5]

Lament: "A passionate expression of grief or sorrow"; "an expression of regret or disappointment; a complaint."[6]

I LOVE TO RUN. Don't hold that against me. One of my friends once commented to me that people who love to run have a couple of screws loose. Maybe I do, or maybe I don't. For me, running is a release. It allows me to create space between my mental and emotional stress and my thoughts. When I run, I'm able to process struggles, fears, and concerns. It is my healthy escape.

Several years ago, I was training for a half-marathon. For those who don't know: A half-marathon is 13.1 miles. This is a significant distance, and I wanted to make sure I was adequately prepared for the task. The rule of thumb for training is to work up to at least half the distance you desire to run, and then at any given time you should be able to easily double that to reach your goal. My first goal was to run three miles consistently and then increase by half a mile every couple of weeks until I got to six and a half miles. Then I could double it and successfully complete the half-marathon. One thing I forgot to mention is that I am extremely competitive, and therein lies my mistake.

I quickly achieved my goal of consistently running three miles a day. I had been doing it for almost a month when I had the bright idea of increasing my speed to see if I could run a ten-minute mile or less. My current pace was about twelve minutes and thirty seconds per mile, so I was certain that I could easily improve my time. Boy, was I mistaken. My first attempt at running three miles in under thirty minutes was going well until I hit the fifteen-minute mark. At around fifteen minutes and twenty seconds I felt a small twinge in my left hamstring. It wasn't at all painful; it just didn't feel right. I should have paid attention to it and slowed down or stopped, but I didn't and instead pushed through, thinking I would "work it out" by continuing to run. Nope! Two minutes later my hamstring seized up and I almost fell off the treadmill in terrible pain. I should have listened to my body, but my stubbornness got the best of me. Now I was sidelined for several weeks with a strained hamstring, the same injury that sidelines even professional football players for weeks.

I should have paid attention to the tension. The minute my hamstring felt different, I should have stopped, stretched, rested, drunk water, and taken a break for a couple of days. It was an indicator that I was pushing my body too hard. We do this with our emotions, too. We ignore the warning signs of a mild disruption, and instead of listening to the tension, we push through and eventually become sidelined with a bigger issue.

Principle #6: Tension is a good thing because it causes us to stop and pay attention to what is happening in the moment.

The basic definition of *tension* is "the state of being stretched tight." Another definition states that tension is "a relationship between ideas or qualities with conflicting demands or implications." I would argue that tension is a mindset, a state of being in which we can hold difficult concepts, ideas, and feelings in the same space without attempting to change or manipulate the outcome. This posture, in turn, stretches and grows us into a more holistic being. How then do we use this concept to grow emotionally?

Learning to Sit with Tension

This might be a novel concept for some and a common one for others. I often get asked, "Why would I want to sit with or within the tension?" It is a good question—why would we want to sit with or sit in something difficult? Because tension can be the wisest teacher. Let me explain.

After my mental-health crisis and passive suicide attempt in sixth grade, I started going to a Christian psychologist who helped me begin to make sense of my small-*t* trauma and the shame that went along with it. I had become very adept at numbing or avoiding my emotions. It was an ordeal to learn to engage with them again (or for the first time). I didn't want to revisit the pain and struggle of my anxiety and depression. It was uncomfortable, and I wanted to avoid it at all costs. My therapist helped me sit with the tension I was feeling. He helped me develop actionable baby steps so that I could create movement out of my struggle and not stay stuck. Reflecting on that experience, I learned a few important things that might help in this conversation.

1. **Tension is uncomfortable.** Let's be honest: Feeling the tension of emotional distress is not fun, nor is it easy. It is important that we call it out for what it is—uncomfortable. But I want you to think about the alternative to sitting

with tension. If we choose to ignore the discomfort of the tension, it begins to back up. The more we ignore it, the more we push it down. The more we push it down, the more pressure builds; eventually it will explode and be a catastrophic mess. If you ignore the "check engine" light on your car for too long, what will happen? Something terrible will happen to the car. The "check engine" light is an indicator pointing to something else. So is emotional tension.

2. **Tension creates opportunity.** If we choose to recognize the uncomfortable nature of tension and sit with it, it has the ability to create opportunity. Opportunity is the "set of circumstances that makes it possible to do something." Recognizing, accepting, and sitting with tension have the potential to propel us forward.

3. **Tension requires us to pause.** Yes! Opportunity is an amazing thing, and if we jump into an opportunity without pausing to reflect on all the nuances of the tension, we have the potential to create a bigger problem than we originally had. Pausing requires us to observe, review, and reflect on the current situation. We must see things as they are and from all angles before we develop a way forward.

4. **Tension requires an action plan.** Pausing for a period of time is good, but if we stay there too long we can get stuck. Opportunity without action is futile. We must find ways to avoid stagnation and move forward. An action plan allows us to evaluate our current circumstances, learn from past successes and failures, and develop a comprehensive way forward. The pausing step and the action step go hand in hand.

5. **Tension moves us to growth.** When we recognize the opportunity presented and choose to pause and develop an action plan, we cannot help but grow. We will either go backward, stay stuck, or move forward. Remember, growth only happens when we go through the process.

Yay! Five steps! This is great, right?! I realize this sounds like a coaching or therapy infomercial: "For only three easy payments of $99.99, I can show you how to put these ideas into action!" Don't worry, I won't do that to you; however, I do realize the need to provide some practical tools to engage in this process well. Here are some of my favorite tools to help process through the tension of emotions. (Note: I will spend an entire chapter on developing emotional language.)

Becoming Old Friends with Your Emotions
Have you ever heard the expression *old friends*? I'm not just talking about the length of a relationship but the depth as well. There are several distinct characteristics of an old friend.

The first characteristic of an old friend is that you are familiar with their features. This is a big one! Why? Because to become an old friend, you need to have extended time with someone. In that extended time, you have a lot of interaction with each other. Through that interaction, you have extensive face-to-face contact and conversations. As you have those conversations, you consciously and unconsciously study your friend's face, eyes, mouth, nonverbals, and so on. As the relationship deepens, you become familiar with the shape of his eyes, his wrinkles, how he smiles or frowns, and his microexpressions. The key here is that familiarity doesn't breed complacency; rather, it breeds depth and intentionality. The more familiar you become with your old friend, the more deeply engaged and comfortable you become.

Another important sign of being old friends with someone is that you aren't surprised by her moods. Let's face it, we can be moody sometimes as we engage and interact with our environments. This mark of an old friend is that we are so familiar with her that the ebb and flow of her moods doesn't surprise us. We recognize what is happening and adjust accordingly, because we have had time and context.

In the same way, we are also not surprised by an old friend's reactions. Have you ever had a friend you've been getting to know, and you think you know him pretty well, but something happens (like he reacts to a situation or something you said) that takes you by surprise? This happens to all of us, and it is a normal component of relationship growth. The mark of an old friend is that you know him well enough, have been around him long enough, and have been present long enough in his life that you've seen and experienced every reaction. Therefore, you are not surprised, confused, or afraid of his reactions.

The pinnacle of close friendship is when you can finish the other person's thoughts and sentences. This is a fun one! Think about why this happens. The amount of time and the diversity of experiences coupled with the intentionality of the relationship syncs you up to her rhythms. My wife and I have been married for more than fifteen years, and this happens to us all the time! It is comical that I say what she's thinking, or she finishes my thought, or we both respond to a situation with the same movie quote. We laugh about it, but there is also something comforting about it! We are known so well that we are synced up in that way.

When you know a friend well enough, you can tell when

something is off, even if he doesn't say anything. This is one of my favorite things about having an old friend. You probably think I am weird, but the I believe that the ability to know someone so well that you can pick up on his energy is an amazing privilege. Our internal moods actually put off quantum energy (if you don't have any idea what I'm talking about, go pick up my book *The Path out of Loneliness: Finding and Fostering Connection to God, Ourselves, and One Another*, where I talk at length about this), and when we are synced up with someone, we then intuitively pick up on those cues and respond accordingly. Essentially, the relationship is so close that there is nowhere he can hide.

For example, my closest friend recently lost his grandmother. He didn't tell me, because he hates talking about stuff like that, but when I called to wish him a happy birthday, I could tell that something was off in his voice. I left it alone. Then a couple of days later, he called to tell me.

"I know," I said.

"You know?" he replied.

"Yes, I heard it in your voice the other day but didn't want to press you on it."

He replied, "Shut up, Marcus," and then he laughed. He knew he couldn't get away with not saying anything, because we know each other well.

Here is the thing: Each of these components requires us to have a deep self-awareness. The better we know ourselves, the better we show up for others. So what in the world does this have to do with our emotions? I'm glad you asked. What if we became old friends with our emotions? How would that change how we act, interact, or react to ourselves and the world around us?

Jason was referred to me by his church. He sought out pastoral care to help him work through his recent diagnosis of type 1 diabetes. His pastor continued to meet with him but thought it would be good for him to receive some clinical support for his anxiety. Jason disclosed that his anxiety, and often panic attacks, would creep up on him, surprise him, and leave him debilitated for several days. As I got to know Jason over a couple of months, I realized that he was unconsciously allowing his anxiety to dictate the rules of his life. Essentially, he was living life without paying attention to the indicators of anxiety and thus allowing it to build to the point that it overwhelmed and blindsided him. This pattern had gone on for several years and was leaving Jason exhausted.

During one session, I stopped Jason midsentence and asked, "What would it look like to become old friends with your anxiety?"

He looked at me with a confused face and replied, "Why on earth would I want to do that?"

"Well, it seems as if you have been a victim of your anxiety, and it might feel different if you had some control over it. Becoming old friends with your anxiety means you have the opportunity to become familiar with its features, you aren't surprised by its moods or reactions, you are able to anticipate its next move, you recognize its symptoms, and you won't be fazed by how it shows up."

Jason sat with my words for a while and then said, "That sounds a bit strange, but I'm open to giving it a shot. Anything could be better than what I've been experiencing."

To make the process easier, I had Jason personify his anxiety. I had him draw his anxiety as if it were a person, and then I had him describe the features, moods, and personality of his personified anxiety. The results were fantastic.

The next session, he came in and exclaimed, "Doc! This was an amazing tool! I was able to manage my anxiety this week and wasn't surprised by it at all." He went on to give me this description of his personified anxiety.

"At first, I didn't know what to draw, but then it started to unfold. He was wearing a Broncos hoodie. The hoodie was two sizes bigger than it needed to be and hid his body, so at first I couldn't determine his size. His face was slightly hidden by the hood, but I could see his profile. His eyes were bright blue, and his smile was mischievous, like he was about to do something to get himself in trouble."

Jason stopped, took a deep breath, and smiled. "Here's the thing, Doc. I thought he was going to be huge, but as I continued to engage in this exercise, I realized the reason the hoodie was two sizes too big was that I was looking at a kid. *A kid!* He couldn't have been much more than four or five years old." I noticed Jason's demeanor change as he told the story.

"Jason," I said, "how has this changed how you look at your anxiety?"

"Well, I think it makes it more manageable, easier to get to know. Instead of this big monster, it's an annoying little kid." The act of personifying his anxiety defused it significantly. It didn't remove it, but helped put it into perspective.

"Okay," I said, "now you have the opportunity to become old friends with your annoying little kid." I took him through the process of how to do this, and after several more sessions, he chose to be done with therapy.

I know this process seems simple, and in many ways it is, but it takes persistence and patience. You have to be willing to engage in the process; you have to be willing to sit with the tension. Here are the basic steps to begin the process of becoming old friends with your emotions.

Step 1: In as many words as possible, describe what your pervasive feeling is.

Step 2: If you were to "see" that emotion represented in physical form, what would it look like? Is it alive? Is it an animal? A human? Describe its features in depth (height, weight, color, what it's wearing, etc.).

Step 3: If you can, draw it. (You do not have to be a good artist to do this.) It is important to bring it to life.

Step 4: Describe its characteristics. Is it annoying? Scary? Moody? Impulsive? Happy? In what ways does this character interact with you?

Step 5: Begin the process of becoming old friends. Sit with it, get to know the nuances of its features. Become a student of its moods and reactions. Get to a place where you can expect its next move. Know how it will respond in various circumstances. Know it well enough that you become comfortable with it no matter what.

Remember, this will not happen overnight. It will take time, perseverance, patience, and practice. I carry a journal with me and write out my thoughts and responses to these steps over time. My personified anxiety and depression are manageable. I am familiar with them. I've embraced the tension they bring, and I allow them the opportunity to teach me and grow me. I have to make sure that I choose to lean into the process, because if I don't make this continual choice, I have the potential to become complacent. And when that happens, I know there can be potential for disaster.

The Practice of Lament

Lament is a spiritual discipline that we don't often discuss in our current Western church culture, but it has significant implications in this conversation about sitting with tension. Lament is defined as "a passionate expression of grief or sorrow," "an expression of regret or disappointment," or "a complaint." I personally use the discipline of lament as a practice to express myself and my emotions more authentically and more deeply. You see, once you've begun the practice of becoming old friends with your emotions, you've opened up the opportunity for authentic depth. The practice of lament is how you get there.

Using the practice of lament will actually enhance your ability to sit with the tension. Sitting with the tension can be a risk, because we are entering into an unknown process that has the potential to hinder our daily functioning (or at least we think it does). Lament is an action-oriented process whereby we actively and intentionally engage with the tension through a guided step-by-step process. By doing this, we provide an opportunity and an avenue to begin to move through the tension rather than stay stagnant in it. Admittedly, this process can feel a bit awkward at first, but as you make it a regular practice or habit, it can and will be a powerful experience. I remember one instance in my personal quiet time when I was walking through this process. The emotional floodgates opened, and I spent the necessary time in tears before God.

As you prepare to lament, make sure you are ready to write from a brutally honest standpoint. We often believe we need to hold back or sugarcoat how we are feeling. Be honest. God can handle it. I will provide you with a step-by-step process of how to lament; however, I want you to use this resource however you see fit. It is important to engage your intellectual, imaginal, sensual (having to do with the five senses), emotional, and relational brain. Use the psalmists as an example—they utilized all aspects of who they were to write their laments. It is also important when writing to use word pictures, metaphors, songs, poems, and so on to describe your current grief, trauma, struggle, or pain. Thinking this way can begin to engage and unlock parts of your brain that need healing.

Step 1: *Identify what you're lamenting.* What grief, trauma, struggle, or pain do you want to lament? Be as specific as possible.

Step 2: *Cry out to God.* How will you talk to him? What needs to change in your relationship with him? What is working in the relationship? What isn't working? Be as specific as possible.

Step 3: *Express your complaint.* What is your chief complaint? What disruption, anger, grief, heartache, or sadness, for example, do you have that needs to be brought to God?

Step 4: *Affirm your trust.* Reflect on your past for a moment. Have you experienced times when it has felt like God was listening or present? Write about them as specifically as possible and affirm your trust in him based on those previous experiences. You don't have to believe or feel this trust currently; you are simply borrowing from past experiences as a reminder.

Step 5: *Petition or request.* What do you want or need from God right now?

Step 6: *Offer additional arguments.* Is there anything else you need to say to God about why he should step in and intervene?

Step 7: *Rage against your enemies.* What people or situations feel like enemies currently? Bring them to God.

Step 8: *Take comfort in the fact that you've been heard.* What do you want or need from God to assure you that he's heard your cry?

Step 9: *Promise to offer praise to God.* What promise can you offer to God about choosing to praise him in the midst of the storm?

Step 10: *Be thankful.* Are there any characteristics of God that you can thank him for in this moment? What person, thing, or situation can you be grateful for?

If you decide to engage with these ten steps to lament, don't just attempt it once. It takes time, intentionality, and practice. If you struggle the first time, it might be tempting to move on with the attitude that it doesn't work. Remember, it takes three cycles of thirty days to implement a new discipline or habit.

Conclusion

I am a firm believer that growth and change happen when we sit with and embrace tension. Being stretched is a good thing, but we must pay attention. If we attempt to "push through" or "get over it," we can very easily become sidelined by a bigger injury. Just like my hamstring sidelined me from my half-marathon training, we can create a more impactful emotional injury if we are not careful.

Recognizing and embracing the tension is the first step in slowing down to begin the process of developing richness and depth in your emotional experiences.

Questions for Reflection

1. Before reading this chapter, what had your experience with tension been?

2. What had your experience with emotional tension been?

3. What was your initial reaction to the conversation about becoming old friends with your emotions? Why did you react that way?

4. Have you ever heard about the discipline of lament? What are your thoughts?

Action Steps

This week, play around with the exercise of becoming old friends with your pervasive emotion. Then start the process of integrating the discipline of lament into your quiet time.

8

ACCEPTANCE IS CRITICAL

Acceptance . . . is when you can look back and say, hey,
I may not be okay with the fact that that happened,
and I may not ever be, but there are new things in my mind
and heart. New things to take my energy and attention.
Things that actually deserve it. Things that don't force me
into having to accept anything I don't want to or move on.
Acceptance is tomorrow. Even if the pain is still there,
you realize it may always be, and somehow, that's okay.

BRIANNA WIEST,
The Truth about Everything

Definitions

Acceptance: "The action of consenting to receive or undertake something offered"; "agreement with or belief in an idea, opinion, or explanation."[1]

Recognition: "Acknowledgment of something's existence, validity, or legality."[2]

Reflection: "A thing that is a consequence of or arises from something else"; "serious thought or consideration"; "an idea about something, especially one that is written down or expressed."[3]

Vulnerability: "The quality or state of being exposed to the possibility of being attacked or harmed, either physically or emotionally."[4]

Openness: "Lack of restriction; accessibility"; "lack of secrecy or concealment; frankness."[5]

I LOVE MY LIFE. Love it! I love being the husband to my amazing wife! I love being the father to my three kids! It is amazing, and it is nothing like I expected. You see, I'm one of those people who likes to make plans, and when I make those plans, I expect those plans to happen the way I plan them. Okay, you can stop laughing now—I am fully aware that this is not how things work. Nevertheless, it took me a great deal of pain and heartache to figure this out.

Sarah and I got married in the fall of 2007. I was a youth and family pastor in the mountains of Colorado, and she was a middle-school teacher. Two months before our wedding I purchased a thousand-square-foot condo in Dillon, Colorado. The place needed work, but it was ours, and it had amazing views. We were set! I thought we were going to put down roots and establish our lives in this beautiful place. Two months after our wedding we found out we were pregnant, and four months after that I found myself in conflict with the church leadership. We were at a crossroads: stay at a job where the leadership was controlling but have a good salary and good benefits or step out in faith and quit my job and go back to school to pursue a degree in counseling.

Obviously, we chose the path of school and counseling, and

we decided to move two months before our first child was born. I went from having a job that paid nearly six figures to working as a shift manager at Chick-fil-A. Our house was still on the market, and our Realtor was confident we would make $80,000 to $100,000 in profit. Then the recession of 2008 hit, and we walked away with one thousand dollars, enough to pay for two semesters of books. My plans were not being fulfilled the way I had hoped. Fast-forward two years, and I was getting ready to graduate with my master's in clinical mental-health counseling. I was excited! No more Chick-fil-A—now I could go back to making real money by opening my own private practice. Three months in, we could barely put food on the table. Once again, my plans hadn't worked out. All the while we were attempting to get pregnant again and felt like we were running up against every barrier possible. I was becoming disillusioned and angry at God, the world, and others. Nothing was working out the way I had planned.

Fast-forward another two years, and I had found a stable job in Colorado Springs working for a community mental-health facility. I was also working as a professor at my alma mater, Colorado Christian University. But we still couldn't get pregnant, and my anger was starting to turn into bitterness toward God and the world. It was Easter, and we had just spent time with Sarah's family in Texas. I left Sarah and Hannah with Sarah's parents for an extended stay while I drove home to go back to work. This was a drive I had made hundreds of times as we'd gone back and forth between Colorado and Texas. I vividly remember driving across northern New Mexico with the sun rising behind me. There were thunderclouds in the sky up ahead, and as the sun came up, what we call "sun doggies" (small rainbow spots) popped up in the sky. As I drove farther and the sun rose higher, the sun doggies would appear and disappear in different places in the sky. As I drove, I got a deep sense in my heart that God was playing with me. This took me by surprise because I had been very turned off to talking with God. I drove a little farther and heard a voice say, "Pray for a baby by Christmas." In that moment it felt like an audible voice, and it freaked me out. I pulled over on the side of the four-lane New Mexico highway, got out of the car, and opened all the doors of my 2004 Honda Pilot. I wanted to make sure there wasn't anyone stowing away in my trunk! I didn't find anyone. I got back in the car and started to drive. Several miles down the road I said out loud, "Okay, Lord! If you want me to pray for a baby by Christmas, I will, but I don't believe you are going to do it. Nothing else has worked out according to plan. Why would this?" It was a skeptical prayer, but I prayed nonetheless.

Two weeks went by, and I had almost forgotten that experience. Sarah and Hannah were home now, but I thought if I told Sarah what had happened, she might think I was going a bit bonkers because I was hearing voices—or I would get her hopes up and nothing would happen again. We had just moved from a small, two-bedroom condo across the complex to a three-bedroom townhome. Boxes were everywhere because we were still attempting to get settled. That particular morning, I woke up and found that I was the only one in bed. This was unusual because I was the morning person and Sarah was the one who always attempted to sleep in. A moment later, Sarah bolted into the room and jumped onto the bed with a pregnancy test.

"Look!" she exclaimed. "I'm pregnant!"

I rubbed my eyes, thinking I was dreaming. "What?" I said in disbelief.

"I'm pregnant!" she repeated.

I was dumbfounded. Could it be true? Could my experience two weeks earlier have prepped my heart and mind for what God had in store? We embraced, cried, and thanked God for his goodness. Elizabeth (Elle) was born on the twenty-sixth of December—a baby for Christmas!

I tell you this story for a couple of different reasons. First, I love to share it because it displays the goodness of God! Second, I share it because it taught me a lot about acceptance. I so desperately wanted to control the outcomes of my life and my future that I was unable to accept what was right in front of me. I was blind to what God was trying to give me, and even more blind to what God was trying to teach me. I wonder how much more I could have grown if I would have (or could have) accepted what God was giving me and teaching me in the moment. I wanted things to happen according to *my* plan and be done *my* way. I was so blinded by my anger with God that I missed out on what he was trying to accomplish.

Principle #7: Accepting our emotions is critical to our maturity.

Pathways to Acceptance

I don't know about you, but I often let my circumstances dictate how I feel or respond emotionally. I tend to fight before I listen. I tend to try to fix before I understand. I have a hard time accepting the here and now, and I have a hard time accepting my emotions in the moment. This has caused me to miss out on a lot of growth opportunities. When we accept our emotions as they are, we open up a posture of learning and growth that is critical to our maturity. Let's take a look at the idea of acceptance from a few different postures:

Posture of recognition: This is an important idea. Why? Because in order to accept our current emotional status, we must first recognize the emotions we are experiencing. Recognition slows us down to a moment in time, forcing us to stay present in the here and now and name what is happening. Recognition means calling out what is actually present and happening. We cannot accept our emotional status if we ignore its existence.

Posture of reflection: A posture of recognition leads to a posture of reflection. Reflection requires us to pause, inspect, ask questions, and be curious. *How did I get here? Where did these emotions come from? How have I handled them in the past? Is this something I can control?* When we properly pause to reflect, we engage in the process of becoming old friends with our emotions; we embrace the tension instead of fighting it.

Posture of vulnerability: Ugh, not that word! Being vulnerable is scary. It requires us to take a risk. *Vulnerability* is defined as "the quality or state of being exposed to the possibility of being attacked or harmed, either physically or emotionally." Read that again. Being vulnerable is an intentional posture of opening ourselves up to the possibility of attack or harm. But it also opens us up to the ability to process and heal. If you think about it, this is an interesting dichotomy. To heal, we must open ourselves up to the possibility of being hurt.

Posture of openness: When we step into vulnerability, we create an opportunity to be open. Being open means finding ways to discuss our emotional processing with others. Growth and acceptance happen in the transparency of being open, and being open allows us the opportunity for accountability. It also gives us a framework to normalize the process and inspire others to explore their own emotional status.

Posture of humility: Being open and vulnerable about our emotional processing also keeps us humble. True humility keeps things out in front, in the open, and in the light of truth. The antithesis to acceptance is pride. Pride tries to control the narrative, whereas openness and vulnerability are fueled by humility. Humility defuses pride and allows an authentic emotional narrative to unfold.

I love to think about emotional acceptance through the lens of postures, because it takes intentional thought and purposeful action to establish and maintain a posture.

The Oil Pump and Self-Awareness

My dear friend and mentor Dr. Wess Stafford and I were enjoying a cup of coffee at one of our routine breakfasts. We were discussing the keys to successful leadership. As we were talking, he paused and looked across the booth. "Mark," he asked, "have I told you about when I used to be a broadcasting student at Biola University?"

"No, I don't think so," I replied as I took a sip of my coffee.

"I was a newbie at this radio station, and I had to drive from Biola to Glendale to fulfill my broadcasting duties. As a newbie I didn't have a set schedule, so I would drive up at different times of the day. Sometimes I would drive up at the crack of dawn, sometimes at midday, sometimes at midnight. I'd drive from Biola through the foothills to Glendale, and littered throughout the foothills were oil pump derricks. There was this one oil pump that I would use as a landmark to confirm that I was only five or so miles from being home. It sounds weird, but over time, that oil pump and I became old friends; it was an indicator that I was almost home to my bed and the safety it brought. I would look for that landmark, I would anticipate it, and I would take a deep breath when I saw it. Without fail it was always there, always pumping. One day I was at home and decided to go for a run in the foothills. Several miles into my run, I realized I had lost track of time and did not know where I was. I saw a hill up ahead and decided to run up it to get my bearings. As I got closer to the top, I heard the most awful screeching sound. As I crested the hill I saw a familiar sight—my oil pump! But something was wrong. The awful screeching sound was coming from my oil pump. I ran up to it to see what was wrong, but I could not get close to it because it was surrounded by a chain-link fence. I pressed up against the fence to see if I could determine what was going on, and I realized it needed maintenance. It needed oil. I moved around to the gate to see if I could get in, but it was locked with a padlock. I couldn't get in. I couldn't help."

Wess paused and sat back in the booth. "This is the same thing I see happening with well-intentioned pastors, leaders, and, well, frankly, people in general. We pour ourselves out serving others and think we are operating well when in fact we are burning out. We are not attending to our own emotional needs, nor are we allowing others close enough to help us make sense of these things. We have a chain-link fence around our hearts, our gates are pad-locked, and we are making an awful screeching sound, but nothing can be done to fix it."

His words stuck with me, and I hope they stick with you, too.

We need to posture ourselves in such a way that we recognize our need. We must reflect on our current status; we must be honest about our emotions, allowing for vulnerability; we must openly discuss our emotions; and we must humbly seek out support as we attempt to navigate the emotional landscape. When we do these things, we begin to tear down the chain-link fences around our hearts and start the healing process. Acceptance must happen first, before anything else.

Questions for Reflection

1. In what ways can you relate to my journey toward acceptance? Have you experienced something similar? In what ways?

2. As you reflect on the postures of acceptance, where are you in the process?

3. Who in your life can you bring into this conversation?

Action Steps

Reflect this week. Reflect on where you are in terms of the postures of acceptance. Reflect on where you want to be, and make a tentative action plan to get there. Begin thinking about who needs to be on this journey with you.

Part Four

THE ART OF
EMOTIONAL
LANGUAGE

9

A THEOLOGY OF SUFFERING AND CARE

The problem of reconciling human suffering with the existence of a God who loves, is only insoluble so long as we attach a trivial meaning to the word 'love', and look on things as if man were the centre of them. Man is not the centre. God does not exist for the sake of man. Man does not exist for his own sake. 'Thou hast created all things, and for thy pleasure they are and were created.' We were made not primarily that we may love God (though we were made for that too) but that God may love us, that we may become objects in which the Divine love may rest 'well pleased'.

C. S. LEWIS, *The Problem of Pain*

Definitions

Theology: "The study of the nature of God."[1]

Suffering: "The state of undergoing pain, distress, or hardship."[2]

Protection: "A person or thing that prevents someone or something from suffering harm or injury."[3]

Care: "The provision or what is necessary for the health, welfare, maintenance, and protection of someone or something."[4]

Compassion: "To suffer with"; from the Latin *compati*: *com* means "with," *pati* means "suffer."[5]

IN MY OPINION, we have it all wrong. We have made things more difficult for ourselves. For some reason, along the way, we decided life should be easy, and when it isn't, we are distraught and despondent. I honestly do not know where this mindset came from or how the church jumped on the health-wealth-prosperity bandwagon, but that is not what I see in the world around me, nor what I read in Scripture. John 15–16 is a perfect example. Here we read that Jesus shared with his disciples that they would be hated by many and that they would be misunderstood and persecuted for the Good News of the gospel. Then he foretold his impending death and said to them, "Do you finally believe? In fact, you're about to make a run for it—saving your own skins and abandoning me. But I'm not abandoned. The Father is with me. I've told you all this so that trusting me, you will be unshakable and assured, deeply at peace. In this godless world you will continue to experience difficulties. But take heart! I've conquered the world" (John 16:31-33).

I love that Jesus didn't sugarcoat this. He blatantly stated, "In this godless world you *will* continue to experience difficulties." This was not a question but a statement, and many scholars read this as a guarantee. So the question in my mind becomes *If this is a guarantee, how do we prepare ourselves, and how do we develop a healthy mindset around this?* Another way to conceptualize it is *What is your developed theology of suffering?* I know, I'm wading into deep theological waters here, but this is a conversation we must have or begin to have. Why? Because as the church, as the body of Christ, if we do not have a developed theology of suffering, we cannot and will not have a comprehensive theology of care, for ourselves or anyone else.

Developing a Theology of Suffering

Before I dive into Scripture, I want you to consider something. How do you view suffering? I know that might be an existential question, but it is an important one. Do you see suffering as a

- form of punishment?
- part of being human?
- consequence of our sin nature?
- result of spiritual warfare?
- all of the above?
- other?

This is not a trick question; it is a genuine one. How we view suffering will directly impact how we care for others and how we care for ourselves. There needs to be balance in this answer. If we lean too far to one side of the conversation, it can be damaging. For example, I was listening to a news excerpt the other day in which a popular prosperity-gospel preacher said that "God won't give you more than you can handle." I'm sure you've heard this phrase and perhaps even assumed that it's somewhere in the Bible. It isn't. This type of thinking negates the impact and importance of suffering and creates a narrative that if I'm suffering (e.g., wrestling with mental and emotional health), something is wrong with me and I am out of favor with God. I could come up with example after example of where we encounter this lie in our society. We must have a right understanding of suffering so we can develop a right understanding of care. Life is hard, and suffering happens (theology of suffering). But when we face difficulties and challenges, God walks with us and strengthens us along the journey (theology of care).

Exploring this further, let me step back a bit. First, we must consider our view of what it means to be human and what it means to be in this world. There are two questions I always ask my counseling students as we wrestle with this topic: *How do you view change?* and *How do you view and understand the human condition?*

Our view of change is something that either keeps us stuck or helps us move forward. If we view suffering as a catalyst for growth and change, we will embrace it rather than see it as a punishment or a roadblock. If we view the human condition as one marred by a gravitational field of sin, brokenness, and spiritual warfare, then we will be able to view suffering holistically as a result of those three components combined (sin: my choice; brokenness: result of the Fall; spiritual warfare: the ongoing struggle).

The caution here is that we must make sure we don't go to extremes in our views. If we view suffering as only punishment, then we will think people are "getting what they deserve," and we won't develop any theology or framework of care. But if we view suffering as something "being done to" people and see them as victims, then we will swoop in and try to rescue them. By trying to rescue them, we won't provide an opportunity for them to wrestle with the struggle, sit with the tension, and grow. There needs to be a balance; there needs to be a choice. Suffering is a lens through which we view emotions and the emotional experience.

Thoughts on Suffering

When it comes to suffering, we can look to Scripture and see that God gives us what I've heard referred to as the three *p*'s: protection, perseverance, and patience. Forgive me for the alliteration! It is easy to remember, and I guess *once a pastor, always a pastor.*

Protection

God, my shepherd!
   I don't need a thing.
You have bedded me down in lush meadows,
   you find me quiet pools to drink from.
True to your word,
   you let me catch my breath
   and send me in the right direction.

Even when the way goes through
   Death Valley,
I'm not afraid
   when you walk at my side.
Your trusty shepherd's crook
   makes me feel secure.

You serve me a six-course dinner
   right in front of my enemies.
You revive my drooping head;
   my cup brims with blessing.

Your beauty and love chase after me
   every day of my life.
I'm back home in the house of God
   for the rest of my life.

PSALM 23

Psalm 23 is such a great passage. It shows me how God views suffering. Now, I may not be fully theologically correct here, but when I read this, I often wonder if the lush meadows and quiet pools are in Death Valley. If they are, it intrigues me that we can find care and relief in a difficult place, which provides an interesting perspective on struggle and suffering. I also notice that the shepherd is always with the sheep. "I'm not afraid when you walk at my side. Your trusty shepherd's crook makes me feel secure." What an amazing visual. Then, moving further in the passage, we see that we are provided a six-course meal in the presence of our enemies. A six-course meal is extravagant and takes a significant amount of time. I have heard this passage quoted over and over throughout my life, but I don't think I've ever sat with the significance of it until recently. Trials will come; of that we are certain. Suffering will happen, but we are instructed not to be afraid because we will not be facing it alone. We can and will find joy and peace in the midst of it, an interesting promise to ponder.

Perseverance

Perseverance is "persistence in doing something despite difficulty or delay in achieving success." James 1:2-4 offers this take on the topic: "Consider it a sheer gift, friends, when tests and challenges come at you from all sides. You know that under pressure, your faith-life is forced into the open and shows its true colors. So don't try to get out of anything prematurely. Let it do its work so you become mature and well-developed, not deficient in any way."

Contextually, James was attempting to edify the early church regarding suffering. He encouraged them to view their trials and troubles differently from the way people outside the church would. Some translations say, "Count it all joy." Joy! *You mean I choose joy in the midst of my suffering?* Yes, it seems that way. Remember, our mindset is everything.

I've been fairly open about our recent struggles as a family. In

2020 my dad almost died from a botched cancer surgery. As he was recovering, Sarah's dad was diagnosed with colon cancer. He's now recovered and cancer free. Then in 2021, my mom was diagnosed with an aggressive form of breast cancer and had to do six months of chemotherapy, which was followed by surgery. During all that, Sarah's fifty-two-year-old aunt died suddenly of blood clots in her lungs. Throughout that entire time, I was also facing major struggles at work (which I previously discussed). It wasn't fun, it wasn't easy, and we didn't always handle it well. However, one of the biggest choices Sarah and I made was to not look at things from a victim mindset. These things were not done to us; they were part of life, and early in the process, we chose joy. Yes, it is easy to say this now, looking back on those two years; however, I can honestly say that I made that conscious choice with my dad in the ICU while he was on life support. In everything, we have a choice. Joy may not be an easy choice, but it is a good one.

Patience

Recognizing our protection and then choosing perseverance might be easy concepts to grasp in this conversation about suffering, but for me, patience is not an easy conversation. Patience is "the capacity to accept or tolerate delay, trouble, or suffering without getting angry or upset." We see this displayed in the story of Job, and that would be the easy story to reference here; however, I'd like to take a different perspective and look at a person who didn't respond well and a God who did, which will lead us to a conversation about a theology of care. I want to talk about Elijah in 1 Kings 19.

The backstory in 1 Kings 18 takes us to the top of Mount Carmel, where Elijah was "battling" the prophets of Baal. He challenged them to a sacrifice on the top of the mountain. He instructed them to build an altar, lay out a sacrifice, and then pray to their gods. The prophets of Baal did this and began calling out to their gods. Nothing happened. They escalated their cries and began to mutilate their bodies to get their gods to respond. Nothing happened. Now it was Elijah's turn. He set up the altar, which consisted of stones, wood, and the spotless sacrifice. He then did something I see as somewhat sarcastic. He drenched the altar in water, so much so that it pooled around the base of the altar. He stepped back from it and prayed. Immediately a ball of fire came down from heaven and consumed the altar. *Everything* was consumed—the stones, the wood, the sacrifice, and the water. The God of Israel, the one true God, appeared and displayed his power and his glory.

Reading this story, I am in awe of God's power and might. God showed up in a spectacular way. But how quickly we forget. In 1 Kings 19 we see that Jezebel was furious that all her prophets were destroyed. She threatened to kill Elijah. Instead of recognizing that the same God who had just consumed the altar with a ball of fire was still good and still powerful, Elijah chose to react out of fear and desperation. I'm not judging at all, because it sounds like the same way I've responded in the past.

Picking the story up in 1 Kings 19:3, we read,

When Elijah saw how things were, he ran for dear life to Beersheba, far in the south of Judah. He left his young servant there and then went on into the desert another day's journey. He came to a lone broom bush and collapsed in its shade, wanting in the worst way to be done with it all—to just die: "Enough of this, GOD! Take my life—I'm ready to join my ancestors in the grave!" Exhausted, he fell asleep under the lone broom bush.

Suddenly an angel shook him awake and said, "Get up and eat!"

He looked around and, to his surprise, right by his head were a loaf of bread baked on some coals and a jug of water. He ate the meal and went back to sleep.

The angel of GOD came back, shook him awake again, and said, "Get up and eat some more—you've got a long journey ahead of you."

I KINGS 19:3-7

Before we move on in this story, I want to point out several key concepts. First, we see that Elijah was human and had short-term memory loss. I say this because it makes me feel better about my past responses. God showed up in a miraculous way and confirmed who he was to Elijah, and then, not a week later, Elijah wanted to die because God wasn't showing up the way he wanted. Second, I want to take a moment to focus on God's response. He could have chastised Elijah's actions and attitudes and reminded him of the recent display of his power on Mount Carmel, but he didn't. He could have used a hurtful tone or reprimanded Elijah for his lack of faith, but he didn't. Instead, he patiently took care of Elijah's immediate needs: two snacks and two naps! I laugh because this is how I respond to my children when they are cranky! God responds to Elijah like a patient father. Amazing!

We pick up the story in verse 8:

He got up, ate and drank his fill, and set out. Nourished by that meal, he walked forty days and nights, all the way to the mountain of God, to Horeb. When he got there, he crawled into a cave and went to sleep.

Then the word of GOD came to him: "So Elijah, what are you doing here?"

"I've been working my heart out for the GOD-of-the-Angel-Armies," said Elijah. "The people of Israel have abandoned your covenant, destroyed the places of worship, and murdered your prophets. I'm the only one left, and now they're trying to kill me."

Then he was told, "Go, stand on the mountain at attention before GOD. GOD will pass by."

A hurricane wind ripped through the mountains and shattered the rocks before GOD, but GOD wasn't to be found in the wind; after the wind an earthquake, but GOD wasn't in the earthquake; and after the earthquake fire, but GOD wasn't in the fire; and after the fire a gentle and quiet whisper.

When Elijah heard the quiet voice, he muffled his face with his great cloak, went to the mouth of the cave, and stood there. A quiet voice asked, "So Elijah, now tell me, what are you doing here?" Elijah said it again, "I've been working my heart out for GOD, the GOD-of-the-Angel-Armies, because the people of Israel have abandoned your covenant, destroyed your places of worship, and murdered your prophets. I'm the only one left, and now they're trying to kill me."

1 KINGS 19:8-14

The story continues with God giving Elijah instructions to go back and link up with Elisha and the remnant of seven thousand believers. Here is what I like about this story and how it relates to our conversation. First, I love how God shows up. Such a good model for us. Second, I love how Elijah responds.

HOW GOD SHOWS UP

The way God shows up tells us a lot about how he views suffering and about how we should respond to suffering.

I find it interesting that right after his display of force on Mount Carmel, God chose to show up in the stillness. He very easily could have shown up in the hurricane, the earthquake, or the fire, but he chose not to. He chose to show up in the sacred stillness. I love this picture because it shows the compassion of God. I honestly didn't understand the weight of this until a friend from Israel asked if I truly understood what the original Hebrew was trying to convey.

He told me, "Mark, the English language often misses out on the depth and beauty of what was trying to be conveyed. When it says God showed up in the stillness or that he showed up in a whisper, what it is saying is that God met Elijah in the stillness of his stillness."

Wow! Sit with that picture for a moment. The almighty Father of heaven and earth, YHWH, valued Elijah and his suffering so much that he chose to meet him in the stillness of Elijah's stillness. *The stillness of his stillness.* Sometimes the English translation of a passage does not even scratch the surface of the intent and beauty of it in the original language. The best way I can conceptualize this statement is by saying that in that moment God met Elijah in the stillness of his own heart. But even as I write this, it doesn't capture the true depth of the picture. God quietly meets Elijah in the center of the prophet's distress and suffering. He isn't loud or boisterous. He is quiet, reflective, and kind. In the center of it, he, God Almighty, brings calm and peace. What a beautiful and sacred view of suffering. I think it is very telling that God views suffering as a part of life. He didn't swoop in and rescue or fix Elijah; he allowed Elijah's suffering to play out and displayed his glory through it.

We see this very posture in Jesus in the Gospels. John 9:1-3 says, "Walking down the street, Jesus saw a man blind from birth. His disciples asked, 'Rabbi, who sinned: this man or his parents, causing him to be born blind?' Jesus said, 'You're asking the wrong question. You're looking for someone to blame. There is no such cause-effect here. Look instead for what God can do.'" Suffering is a vehicle for God's glory to be displayed.

HOW ELIJAH RESPONDS

Elijah's response is not complicated. It is a direct result of how God chose to show up. After Elijah was able to get his frustrations out, after he was listened to, and after he was given instruction, he responded with obedience.

When someone shows up to our experience without judgment or condemnation, without trying to fix or overspiritualize it, it opens up a pathway for care. When we show up this way, we disarm the individual. The way God showed up allowed Elijah the opportunity to be heard. If God had showed up any other way, Elijah might have become defensive. When we show up this way with others, it allows them the opportunity to move from deregulation to regulation, from active suffering into the process of healing and care.

A Theology of Care

I don't know about you, but when I think about care, it is always external. I'm caring for someone else. The thought-provoking thing is that we can only care for others as much as we have cared for ourselves. Think about that for a moment. We can only care for others as much as we have cared for ourselves. This is why the conversations in this book are so important, and this is why I devote an entire chapter to the idea of developing emotional language. We must begin with a right and developed understanding of our emotions and a right and developed understanding of suffering. Only then can we create a comprehensive theology of care.

It takes a balanced, healthy love of self for this to work. The greatest commandment, found in Matthew, tells us to "'love the Lord your God with all your passion and prayer and intelligence.' This is the most important, the first on any list. But there is a second to set alongside it: 'Love others as well as you love yourself.' These two commands are pegs; everything in God's Law and the Prophets hangs from them" (22:37-40). The part translated "set alongside it" is the Greek word *homoios,* which means "equal to." So I read this as saying that we need to have a healthy relationship with God, a healthy relationship with others, and an equally healthy relationship with self, all held together by the triune God (see the figure below). This is significant to our conversation about a theology of care because we must first find ways to wrestle with and care for ourselves. We must develop a compassion for self so we can have compassion for others.

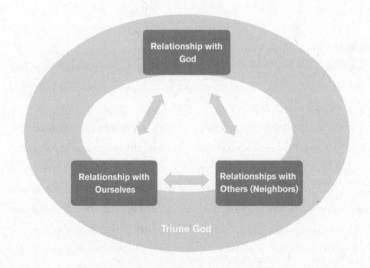

Principle #8: Compassion is not optional.

When you hear the word *compassion*, what is your first thought? My mind always goes to care and concern. But what if I told you that the definition of *compassion* is actually "suffering with" in Latin? The Latin root word *compati* is a combination of *com* ("with") and *pati* ("suffer"). This completely changes my perspective on the idea of compassion. It now requires something of us.

True self-compassion requires us to sit with difficulties, trials, painful and/or uncomfortable emotions, and suffering and work through them. Basically, everything we've been discussing up to this point. Once we've wrestled with our own story, we can honestly and effectively have compassion for others. The more familiar our suffering is to us, the more comfortable we can be when we sit with others in their struggles. I hope this realization opens your eyes to the bigger conversation. It completely changes the way I see God, others, and myself.

Creating an Effective Model of Care

I was a good student in school, but I often lacked creativity. Give me an example or a template, and I could get creative within the prescribed framework. Sometimes I feel the same way when it comes to developing a theology of care. Give me an example or a model, and I'll be okay. Most of the time it isn't that simple, but I believe we have an amazing model in the person and ministry of Jesus Christ. I often tell my clinical mental health master's students at Colorado Christian University that what we get to do each day as counselors is a direct representation of the mission and work of Jesus.

Let's look at the example in Isaiah 61. This was a prophecy of the ministry of Jesus, fulfilled in the Gospel of Luke. I believe it provides a solid foundation for a theology of care.

> The Spirit of GOD, the Master, is on me
>   because GOD anointed me.
> He sent me to preach good news to the poor,
>   heal the heartbroken,
> Announce freedom to all captives,
>   pardon all prisoners.
> GOD sent me to announce the year of his grace—
>   a celebration of God's destruction of our enemies—
>   and to comfort all who mourn,
> To care for the needs of all who mourn in Zion,
>   give them bouquets of roses instead of ashes,
> Messages of joy instead of news of doom,
>   a praising heart instead of a languid spirit.
> Rename them "Oaks of Righteousness"
>   planted by GOD to display his glory.
> They'll rebuild the old ruins,
>   raise a new city out of the wreckage.
> They'll start over on the ruined cities,
>   take the rubble left behind and make it new.
> You'll hire outsiders to herd your flocks
>   and foreigners to work your fields,
> But you'll have the title "Priests of GOD,"
>   honored as ministers of our God.
> You'll feast on the bounty of nations,
>   you'll bask in their glory.
> Because you got a double dose of trouble

and more than your share of contempt,
Your inheritance in the land will be doubled
   and your joy go on forever.
ISAIAH 61:1-7

- **Preach good news to the poor.** This is pretty straightforward. Good news is different from the news they've heard before. It is intended to change mindset and perspective. The word *poor* here can be linked to the "poor in spirit" mentioned in the Beatitudes (see Matthew 5:3, ESV). A true theology of care starts with good news.

- **Heal the heartbroken.** The ESV translates this as "bind up the brokenhearted." This is powerful imagery. Have you ever needed a splint or a cast? A broken bone needs to be stabilized and given strength from something outside itself so that it can properly heal. In the same way, a theology of care must provide added strength from outside so that the heartbroken can heal. Outside strength binds up and lends itself to the process of healing, both internally and externally.

- **Announce freedom to all captives.** *Liberty* is defined as "the state of being free within society from oppressive restrictions imposed by authority on one's way of life or behavior." What a cool analogy for a theology of care that shouts, *It doesn't have to be this way! You can live in freedom!* What is unique here is that this is not a private conversation. To *proclaim* means to "officially declare publicly." When we step into a theology of care, we are privately and publicly declaring freedom. I like this because it doesn't leave any room for misinformation or manipulation. If something has been publicly declared, the same message has gone out to everyone.

- **Pardon all prisoners.** Repeating and emphasizing the previous statement ("announce freedom to all captives") is a result of the proclamation.

- **Announce the year of God's grace and his destruction of our enemies.** We stand up and fight for the oppressed, the poor, and the heartbroken.

- **Comfort all who mourn.** This is a "duh" statement. Of course a theology of care requires comfort, but I don't think it is in the way you are accustomed to. We often default to comforting with words. What if I were to tell you that comforting with words actually doesn't do much? Only 10 percent of our communication happens through words. The remainder happens with our presence. To truly comfort, we need to be okay with ourselves, with pain, with sadness, and with struggle, and we need to be okay with silence, with awkwardness, and with not being able to fix the situation. As I discussed earlier, this is where our mirror neurons come into play. The more secure and comfortable we are with ourselves and our emotional experiences, the greater comfort we can provide.

- **Give them bouquets of roses instead of ashes, messages of joy instead of news of doom, a praising heart instead of a languid spirit.** A true theology of care helps alter thinking, replacing unhealthy mindsets with healthy ones. I like the images here because the care offered doesn't simply cover up what is going on but completely replaces it with something else.

When we read the remainder of this passage through verse 7, we see the results. There will be a rebuilding from the ruins, a double inheritance will be given, shame will be wiped out, and there will be everlasting joy. Developing a theology of suffering leads us to a practical theology of care. When we have developed a theology of care, we will be able to invite people into the process of emotional growth, maturity, and wellness.

Questions for Reflection

1. What is your personal view of suffering?

2. What are your thoughts about a theology of suffering?

3. Do you agree with my statement that we must have a theology of suffering before we have a theology of care? If not, why?

4. What are your thoughts on compassion? How have they changed with this new understanding?

5. What are your thoughts on an effective model of care?

Action Steps

This is a heavy topic that requires us to pause and take stock of our own ideologies. Take some time to think about suffering and care. How have you had compassion for yourself? Where do you need to reevaluate?

10

DEVELOPING YOUR
EMOTIONAL LANGUAGE

*Emotions change how we see the world and how we interpret
the actions of others. We do not seek to challenge why we are
feeling a particular emotion; instead, we seek to confirm it.*

PAUL EKMAN,
*Emotions Revealed:
Understanding Faces and Feelings*

Definitions

Language: "The principal method of human communication,
consisting of words used in a structured and conventional
way and conveyed by speech, writing, or gesture."[1]

Meaning: "What is meant by a word, text, concept, or
action"; "implied or explicit significance"; "important or
worthwhile quality; purpose."[2]

Depth: "The quality of being intense or extreme"; "complexity and profundity of thought"; "extensive and detailed study
or knowledge."[3]

EMOTIONS ARE CONFUSING, but they can be a great teacher if we allow them to be. The problem is that many of us don't have effective language to put to our experiences. Remember, emotions are a neurophysiological sensation that we feel and then make (or attempt to make) cognitive sense of based on our language and experience. This can be difficult because all of us have had different emotional experiences and many of us have not been given the proper language to process them. If those experiences have been traumatic, then we truly cannot put language to them because the Broca's area of the brain, which is associated with speech, gets hijacked and has difficulty making sense of them. So the question becomes *How do we develop emotional language?* or, as the current trend dictates, *How do we develop emotional intelligence?* (Note: I will circle back to emotional intelligence in this chapter because, in my opinion, you cannot have emotional intelligence until you have emotional language.)

How do you develop emotional language? I'm glad you asked! My question to you is this: Are you ready to do the work? Up to this point, we've discussed a bunch of different ways we try to ignore, numb, or avoid, and the specific consequences therein, and I've challenged you to consider where you are in this process. Now I want you to take the next step and begin to explore your emotions. Remember, there are neither good nor bad emotions; there are just emotions. They indicate where we are and provide specific opportunity for growth.

I vividly remember my first fight with my friend Christopher. I had two friends growing up in California named Christopher. This Christopher also lived around the block from me, but in a different direction from the other Christopher (the one whose home I'd attempted to spend the night in). I went to a Christian school with this Christopher, and we were great friends. At the time of this story, I think we were in the second or third grade. One day, Christopher and I were doing a group art project, and we couldn't agree on a color. I was trying to express my thoughts, and he went ahead and did what he wanted to do. I got really mad and pushed him just hard enough that he stumbled back and tripped over the desk and fell. I don't remember if he hurt himself, but I do remember getting in trouble.

Our teacher, Ms. Crow, was kind but firm, and she came down to my level and asked what had happened. I told her my side of the story, Christopher told her his side of the story, and then she asked me what I'd been thinking when I'd pushed him. I responded with "I don't know."

I remember the sensation of anger rising up the back of my neck to the top of my head. I remember getting teary-eyed, gritting my teeth, and immediately reacting to my situation but not having language to put to it. I wish Ms. Crow had said something like "By your action of pushing Christopher, you are telling me that you are mad." That would have helped me figure it out, but it was also more than that. Yes, I was mad, but I was mad because I didn't feel heard, I was being dismissed, and my opinion didn't seem to matter. But I couldn't communicate that because I didn't have the language for it, and Ms. Crow didn't know how to help me process. I was mad, and I reacted. Sound familiar? I'm sure it does. But it doesn't have to be this way.

I mentioned earlier that humans are born with the capacity for emotions such as joy, happiness, fear, and shyness; however, those emotions are only developed through specific and intentional nurturing. In the same way, we develop a comprehensive emotional language through our models, our experiences, and our nurturing. We must tap into our own personal emotional narrative and reflect on our own experiences. It is important to note that this process should not be done alone in an echo chamber or a silo. Many of us have experienced difficult circumstances in our lives, and some of us have experienced trauma. If this is your first time exploring your emotions at this level, I would encourage you to partner with a licensed therapist and/or a certified life coach. If you are not fully prepared, this process can be overwhelming—it does not replace counseling, so adequately prepare yourself. (In the next couple of sections I will use myself as an example. Once you read through the example exercises, I will then walk you through your own processing.)

I've always struggled with anxiety. I'm not ashamed to talk about it. I've worked through it, learned from it, grown, matured, and developed resiliency and grit. I want these things for you, too. One thing I've had to realize is that anxiety is a complex experience. Dealing with the anxiety itself would feel overwhelming, and I would often feel paralyzed, unable to act. It wasn't until I was able to dive into the nuances of my anxiety that I realized it was a mixture of fear, sadness, joy, anticipation, worry, and panic. When I became able to put words to my anxiety in that way, I then became able to start the process of becoming old friends with my emotions. So how did I do that? Here are a number of practical activities I've used that will jump-start the process for you.

Mapping Your Emotions: Where Do You Feel Them in Your Body?

We feel everything. Our bodies are designed to respond to both internal and external stimuli. An emotion is a neurophysiological response to those stimuli. We attempt to make meaning from that feeling by accessing our language and our previous experiences. The difficulty lies in putting language to our experiences. Here are the five major or universal emotions and how they are felt physically and conceptualized cognitively.[4]

1. **Mad:** When anger manifests in the body, it is felt in the head, neck, shoulders, lungs, arms, and hands. It is typically a tingly feeling and/or a hot wave that comes over you. It makes it feel like you want to react impulsively by fighting or running. When anger hits, your body goes into protective mode, and the volume of blood that goes to help your brain function is redirected to your major organs and extremities for fight, flight, or freeze.

2. **Sad:** Sadness feels like negative energy or energy leaving the body. It has been described as an intense heaviness, almost as if your extremities are being weighed down by an internal force. There is a heaviness of the heart and a coldness that consumes the body.

3. **Glad:** Happiness is an interesting emotion. It is felt throughout the entire body. It is centered around the heart and head and makes you feel like you are filled with helium, ready to take flight. Your body feels light and airy, with positive energy radiating through it.

4. **Scared:** In some ways, the feeling of fear is similar to sadness in that it drains the body of movement and energy; however, there is a more intensified feeling in your core that can feel like butterflies in the stomach, a racing heart, or the inability to catch your breath.

5. **Disgusted:** Disgust is centered in your throat and gut. It has been said that disgust is the only core emotion that has

a taste. If you feel disgust, you may have an upset stomach or feel like something is stuck in your throat.

These are universal descriptions of the core emotions, based on hundreds of thousands of self-reports and the use of a theoretical framework called somatic psychotherapy, which focuses directly on the body's experiences. Can you relate to these descriptions? Which ones have you felt recently? As you begin to learn more about your emotions, try to recognize and put language to your body's experience.

Float Back

First, a disclaimer: *If you have experienced significant trauma of any kind and have not worked through it or recognized it at all, do not commit to this activity. This activity is intended to provide clarity and insight into where your pervasive emotion is coming from. It also provides a way you can begin to make sense of it. If you have unresolved or undiscovered trauma, seek out a licensed therapist.*

The "float back" activity requires you to do a couple of things. First, make sure you are in a safe, quiet place. If you are not, then don't continue. Once you're in that safe, quiet place, take a deep breath (or two) to ground yourself and quiet your mind. Next, tap into your primary feeling, the feeling you experience most of the time. Tapping into my anxiety is easy because it is a feeling I am very familiar with. Once you've tapped into your feeling, focus on where it is manifesting in your body. I feel my anxiety in three places: my stomach, my chest, and my shoulders. I cannot settle my stomach, I cannot catch my breath, and my shoulders start to tingle.

Once you've tapped into where you feel it in your body, ask yourself this question: *When was the first time I ever felt this?* After asking yourself this question, sit with it for a while and begin to pay attention to what thoughts or memories arise. Write down those thoughts and memories in a journal. What was the scenario? What was the feeling? What story did you tell yourself about the scenario or feeling?

The first time I did this activity as I began to explore my anxiety, I was transported back to the memory I shared earlier, when I went to school with my fuzzy slippers on instead of my shoes. It sparked a narrative of fear, lack of control, insecurity, sadness, and panic. As I allowed those feelings to unfold, I realized they were all the same feelings I wrestled with in the present. I wrote down the story and the associated emotions and began the process of becoming familiar with them. In some ways the immediate response to the activity was relief because it had allowed me to put language to how I had felt and created a tangible representation of what and how I was feeling presently.

Emotions Worksheet

This next activity will help you explore your emotions in a different way. I created this several years ago to help individuals develop more comprehensive language around their emotions. Scan this QR code to download a worksheet. I will walk you through it here, and you can try it for yourself later.

The Emotions Worksheet is based on the five senses and a series of questions to help develop a broader and deeper understanding of your emotion. I will again use my anxiety as an example.

At the top of the worksheet, I would write down *anxiety* as my pervasive emotion and then turn to the next page. The first question is "If I could taste my anxiety, what would it taste like?" I would answer that easily: If I could taste my anxiety, it would taste like moldy fruit. The next question on the first page is "If I was dealing with the taste of moldy fruit, how would that make me feel?" Using the emotions wheel,[5] I would choose a first-level emotion from the first circle. My emotion would be *disgusted*. Staying in the same pie as *disgusted*, I would then move to the second circle and choose a second-level emotion. My emotion would be *repugnance*. Then I would move to the third circle of the same pie and choose the third-level emotion *nauseated*. I would then go through the same process for *Touch*, *Smell*, *Visual*, and *Auditory*.

Once completed, I would have fifteen descriptive emotional words—five first-level emotion words, five second-level emotion words, and five third-level emotion words. Then I would go back and circle the first-level emotion word I most relate to, the second-level emotion I most relate to, and the third-level emotion I most relate to. Once that's completed, I'd take my original feeling word and add three new descriptors.

Now I'd have words to describe how I really felt. Furthermore, I'd now have greater understanding of how my anxiety affects me, which corresponds with how my anxiety can make me feel physiologically.

Emotions Wheel

I like the emotions wheel because it helps create and develop a much deeper understanding of how complex our emotions can be. As I discussed in the description of the Emotions Worksheet activity, the emotions wheel is broken down into three circles. The central circle consists of our primary universal emotions—*mad, glad, sad, disgusted,* and *scared*. From there they branch out into five separate pies as you move from the first circle to the second circle, and then to the third circle. Each level provides more depth and richness to your original first-level emotion.

I feel . . .

Inner ring: disgusted, scared, mad, glad, sad

scared: nervous, anxious, surprised, desperate, panic, horror, terror, exasperated, argumentative

mad: bitter, vengeful, furious, critical, upset, hopeful

scared (outer): timid, shocked, stunned, insignificant, unsatisfied, overwhelmed, worried, dread, jumpy, hysterical, exposed, frustrated, mean, insecure, threatened, sarcastic, violated, provoked, hostile, irritated, grumpy, suspicious, jealous, hurt, annoyed

glad: creative, energetic, ecstatic, excited, wonder, prideful, peaceful, miserable, despair

glad (outer): thankful, optimistic, fascinated, sensuous, stimulated, playful, cheerful, joyful, aroused, loving, compassionate, amused, powerful, courageous, content, relief, discouraged, fragile, lonely, isolated, empty, vulnerable, disappointed, depressed, agonized, distraught, hopeless, helpless, resigned

sad: grief, sorrow, anguish, powerless

disgusted: shame, distaste, repugnance, revulsion, abhorrence, loathing

disgusted (outer): guilt, awful, embarrassed, aversion, nauseated, horrified, hesitance, judgmental, disapproving, dislike, contempt, trepidation, disillusioned

129

As you develop your emotional intelligence and emotional language, the emotions wheel will give you more than enough information to use as you broaden your vocabulary. I use it, and I encourage my clients to use it. If they don't know what a word means, I have them look it up in the dictionary and write the definition in their journal.

Emotion Faces

Sometimes words don't cut it and you need a visual. The emotion faces[6] provide added value and depth to the conversation. I am a visual person, and it helps to see what a particular emotion might look like. This increases both awareness and understanding. I specifically like the emotion faces because they offer a great way to have emotions modeled to you.

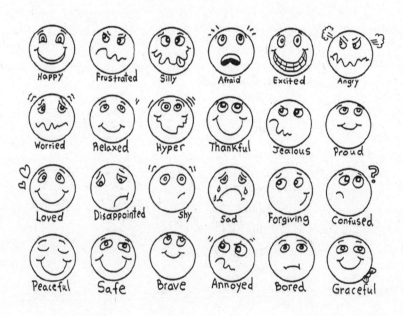

As previously discussed, the primary way we learn about emotions is through the modeling of our primary caregivers. If we had poor models, we don't have those emotional paradigms integrated into our experiences, and as a result, we struggle to make sense of our own internal emotional world as well as the external emotional world around us.

Meaning Making

Meaning making is an important step in the process toward emotional wholeness. It is when we develop meaning that we truly experience freedom from being controlled by our emotions and move to a place where we can interact with our emotions as tools and integrate them into the fabric of our daily lives. This is where the process becomes beneficial and, dare I say, fun. I like asking myself these two questions as I work toward meaning making:

1. What stories am I telling myself about my emotions or my emotional experiences?

and

2. What stories are my emotions actually trying to communicate?

Differentiating between these two questions is important for exploring and engaging in what is actually going on versus what is perceived to be happening.

As I am sitting here at my desk in Monument, Colorado, I am experiencing an emotional upset. We are in the process of selling our home and moving to a different state. Everything was going smoothly until today, when we hit a speed bump that could derail the entire process. Of course, when something happens that doesn't fit within your plans or paradigm, you react. I reacted. But I reacted with a story about myself (question one above). My story is about how I don't deserve nice things or don't deserve for things to go smoothly. I caught myself starting to spiral.

Then about halfway through the day, I realized I was falling back into my old emotional-story patterns. I quickly stopped and readjusted. I walked through my emotional development exercises and realized the actual story my emotions were telling (question 2 above). They were telling me that this situation was hard, wasn't fair, put me in an out-of-control mindset, worried me, made me scared—and that there was absolutely nothing I could do about it. I then was able to use an Emotional ANI (Affirming, Negative, Interesting/Informational) chart to help me process these feelings further. This is a tool my daughter, Hannah, uses in her classical education to brainstorm thoughts and ideas. I found it to be very helpful for my emotional storytelling process. Let me walk you through it:

> **Purpose:** Helping create a framework for emotions so that when you face an easy or difficult emotion you can use this process to evaluate the emotion itself and then examine how you handled the emotion.
>
> **Step 1:** Name the emotion you feel.
>
> **Step 2:** Explore the affirmative or figure out the positive about the emotion. This might take work and insight if this is a difficult or painful emotion. But remember, the goal is growth.

Step 3: Explore the negative or difficult components of the emotion. What about this emotion is hard? What is painful? Remember to write this all out in a narrative form.

Step 4: Write out what you find interesting about the emotion. Take a step back and view it from a distance. What information is out there about it? Create a definition and learn as much as you possibly can about the emotion.

Now let's use this to evaluate how you handled the emotion.

Step 1: Write out what happened.

Step 2: In what ways did you respond well? Affirm yourself? You want this to be repeated in the future.

Step 3: In what ways did you react poorly? Why? What could have been done differently? Be honest!

Step 4: What did you learn about yourself? What did you learn about the experience?

These activities may feel overwhelming and awkward at first, but I know they work. They have been beneficial tools in my life and the lives of my clients for many years. The key here is to stick with it, to be patient, and to persevere.

The Rule of Thirds

After years of watching people in my practice, I developed a "rule of thirds." It goes like this: I tell my clients at the start of therapy, "One-third of my clients will have a heavens-opening-up, miraculous experience; one-third of my clients will experience sustainable small changes (kind of like watching your kids grow—you don't realize how much they've grown until you see them through the eyes of someone else); and one-third of my clients will see no change at all."

I then pause, look at my client, and ask, "What is the factor that causes these varied results?" Typically, my client will sit there awhile and then say something like "My participation" or "My mindset" or "My willingness to work" or "My willingness to change." These all represent the correct answer. The rule of thirds applies to this conversation too. Which one will you be?

Emotional Dissonance versus Emotional Resonance

I don't want to belabor the point, but let's talk about emotions and your emotional journey in one more way: through the idea of dissonance and resonance.

Dissonance is "a tension or clash resulting from the combination of two disharmonious or unsuitable elements." Something is not working or fitting together properly, and it has created tension. Remember, tension is not a bad thing; it is an indication. So when we have emotional dissonance, something is out of alignment or off, and we need to pay attention.

Even if you don't have the emotional language yet, you can still recognize when your mental and emotional status is in dissonance. Yes, this takes awareness and practice, and in my fifteen years of being a counselor, I haven't yet met someone who didn't recognize when something was off. The question was whether they stopped to figure out what was going on or chose to just ignore the signals.

On the other end of the spectrum is resonance. Resonance is "the quality in a sound of being deep, full, and reverberating; the ability to evoke or suggest images, memories, and emotions."

I see emotional resonance as congruence, meaning that our heart, mind, soul, and body are in alignment.

Please hear me on this: It doesn't mean that things are smooth, or perfect, or even easy; it means that you've made the effort and done the work to understand what emotions you are experiencing, why you are experiencing them, the stories behind them, and the language they evoke. You are aware of what is going on and why it is going on, and you are able to communicate those things and develop a productive way forward. Doing this work will help you live within a range of a "healthy" emotional resonance.

Creating Depth

I love nature. I love being out in the forest, by a river, in the mountains, or by the ocean. Anything to do with nature, I love it. One of my favorite passages of Scripture is Isaiah 61:3. I love it so much I have it tattooed on my forearm. It says, "Rename them 'Oaks of Righteousness' planted by GOD to display his glory."

This is a beautiful picture, because oaks have depth. Their roots go deep, they are robust in size, and they shield or shelter a large area. One thing I've noticed about certain types of oaks, especially oaks from California and live oaks in the South, is that they don't show up in a dense forest. Instead, they are out in the open or grouped with two to three others in a grove. I was fascinated when I realized this, and I started to do more research. What I discovered was profound. Trees protected in a dense forest do not develop a deep root system. They don't need to, because there is little to no adversity in the weather. It is the tree that is standing out in the open or in a small grove that has weathered the storm that has depth and strength. Its roots go deep.

This beautiful metaphor is for you. You may think you want

to be protected because it feels safe and easy, but in all actuality, it is keeping you from depth and from strength. It is the storm that refines you. When you face difficult and painful emotions and you've done the prework, you have the opportunity to lean in, to grow, to develop resiliency and grit. And then you can become a strong, powerful, sensitive, and compassionate force in your own life and the lives of others.

Questions for Reflection

1. Where are you in your emotional language development?

2. What experiences have contributed to your emotional language?

3. Where do you feel like you excel?

4. Where do you feel like you struggle?

5. When it comes to the rule of thirds, which one do you identify with most? Why?

6. What are your initial thoughts about the various exercises?

Action Steps

This is your chance to practice and grow. I have given you a lot of opportunities throughout this book to reflect; now it is time to engage. Work through each of these activities, then begin to share your growth experiences with others! Remember, we grow and change best in a safe and supportive community.

CONCLUSION

WHOLENESS IS AN AMBIGUOUS CONCEPT. Trying to attain it can feel like chasing a dream. It would be amazing to have a perfect emotional life, but is this truly realistic? Complete wholeness isn't attainable this side of heaven, but Scripture says we can experience aspects of wholeness as we work, strive, and pay attention to integral things in our lives.

The intention of this book is to shake things up, to highlight the blatant inconsistencies in our emotional lives and the outright lies that are being propagated in our world and even the church. Beyond that, it is a challenge to you personally. Things do not have to continue the way they always have. You have the power to alter how current and future generations experience, engage with, and interact with emotions.

Clarity clears confusion. This is certain and absolute, and it requires intentionality, purpose, and persistence. As we wrap up our time together, I want you to reflect on three key things:

1. What needs to be **cleared** in your life?
2. What do you want to **create** in the newly cleared space?
3. What do you need to **cultivate** from what was created?

Clear

I honestly did not understand the complexity of the verb *clear* until I moved to Southeast Texas. If you've been to East Texas or Southeast Texas, you know that the landscape is beautiful. It is lush, green, and vibrant. And it is full of trees, plants, vines, and undergrowth. In some portions of the forest, you can't see two feet in—it is that dense! Clearing land to build a home takes a lot of time and effort. You can't just cut down the trees and shrubs; you have to uproot everything. Why? If you don't, these plants will grow back, affecting the foundation of the house as they do. Clearing the forest also requires tilling the soil so you're ready to build and plant.

This is the visual I want you to have as you reflect on your journey through this book. Open up your journal and pull out the exercises. What stands out in your narrative? What things in your life have been cleared or need to be cleared to make room for a solid emotional foundation?

Create

Creativity, the act of creating something different or new, is a beautiful reflection of the triune God within us. When we develop something new, we are living out our best, most authentic selves. We don't often talk about this as a society or church, but it's important to consider. When you intentionally and purposefully clear things out of your life, you leave space for something new.

So what do you want to create? What *should* you create? On this journey toward mental and emotional wholeness, it is essential to replace old, broken ways of operating with healthy, creative ways of living. That's how we move from merely surviving to positively thriving. In John 10:10 Jesus promises: "I came so they can have real and eternal life, more and better life than they ever dreamed of." This promise is also a choice. Life is full of big and small choices, each one with positive and/or negative consequences. As we navigate the choices we encounter, we also decide how to respond to Jesus' promise. When we clear space for something new and are offered a better life, it becomes *our choice* how to interact with that. What do we create amid the promise of an abundant life? It comes down to altering our emotional mindsets, one response at a time. The situation may not change, but how we engage in it can change. This is where a new creation begins.

Consider what needs to be created in your life and what you want to create. Make a choice right now, follow through, and don't give up! Remember, it takes three cycles of thirty days to create something that lasts. After each cycle it becomes easier and easier to operate within your new creation, until it becomes second nature. Becoming our best selves doesn't happen overnight. It takes time, intentionality, practice, persistence, focus, and informed choices.

Cultivate

The last step in this process is finding ways to cultivate what you've created. When I think of the process of cultivating something, I think of gardening. I love working in the garden. And I particularly love roses. But roses are finicky. You can't just plant a rosebush and hope for the best. If you do, it will eventually die (even if you water and fertilize it regularly). If you want your roses to thrive, you'll regularly test the soil's pH level, trim the rosebush's branches, and remove old, dead flowers. If your rosebush isn't cultivated in this way, it won't survive—and it certainly won't thrive. This same concept applies to what you've read in this book. You can learn new ways of dealing with your emotions, clear out old, unhealthy habits, and create new emotional models, but if you don't cultivate what you've created, it will eventually die. So how *do* you cultivate what you've learned and established?

> **Step 1:** Write it out! Take time to write out what you've learned, what you've cleared, and what you've created. When you write it out, it becomes real. It activates parts of the brain that simply thinking about these things won't, and it starts to lay a new neural pathway (that magical three cycles of thirty days). It is also a great way to keep yourself accountable. You might even tape what you write to the refrigerator or a mirror so you're regularly reminded of your choice toward the abundant life Jesus offers.
>
> **Step 2:** Share it with a trusted person. I wouldn't suggest sharing it with the world, but is there a friend, family member, pastor, or counselor you can share this process with? When you share your creation, it becomes real and actionable—and bigger than yourself. Sharing also fosters accountability.
>
> **Step 3:** Practice! This may feel awkward, but if you've created new ways of experiencing or expressing emotions, they won't be second nature yet, so practice and adjust until they become

part of who you are. I'm not saying to fake it till you make it but rather to fake it till you *become* it.

Step 4: Never stop learning and growing. Did you know that the brain is the only organ that doesn't have to deteriorate with age? We can make new neural connections until the day we die. This means that we can clear, create, and cultivate new ideas and concepts indefinitely! What do you want to learn next about emotions and mental health? Go research it!

Clearing, creating, and cultivating collide into a messy embrace when we allow a theology of care to develop out of a theology of suffering. As we journey toward healing, toward Christ, and toward wholeness, we must understand that everyone's healing looks different and everyone's healing might be messy as they sort out their emotions, hurts, and uncertainties. It's worth it! Stay on the path to wholeness. You won't be disappointed with where it leads.

ABOUT THE AUTHOR

DR. MARK MAYFIELD is an author, speaker, leadership coach, licensed professional counselor (LPC), and professor. He has extensive experience in executive leadership as the founder and former CEO of Mayfield Counseling Centers, a 501(c)(3) nonprofit in Colorado Springs with over twenty-five thousand appointments a year as well as from helping churches and organizations navigate the complexities of mental and emotional health. Clinically, Dr. Mayfield is an expert in working with families affected by trauma. He is an assistant professor of clinical mental-health counseling at Colorado Christian University, the director of practice and ministry development for the American Association of Christian Counselors (AACC), and the editor of *Marriage and Family: A Christian Journal*.

Dr. Mayfield is the author of three books: *Help! My Teen Is Self-Injuring: A Crisis Manual for Parents*, which addresses his own suicide survival story and provides practical tools to help a child who may be struggling; *The Path out of Loneliness: Finding and Fostering Connection to God, Ourselves, and One Another*; and *The Path to Wholeness: Managing Emotions, Finding Healing, and Becoming Our Best Selves.*

He has been featured in prominent media outlets, including *Woman's Day*, HelloGiggles, NBC, *Reader's Digest*, *Byrdie*, and more. Dr. Mayfield is on a list of mental-health professionals who were invited to the White House in December 2019 and has had periodic calls with the White House to discuss mental health in America.

Dr. Mayfield is currently working on research in equine-facilitated psychotherapy with veterans and in social justice and the church.

Dr. Mayfield lives in Texas with his wife of fifteen years and their three children.

For more information on Dr. Mark Mayfield, check out his website and follow him on social media.

drmayfield.com

 @thedrmayfield

 @thedrmayfield

NOTES

1 | THE NEED FOR LANGUAGE
1. Lexico, s.v. "principle, *n.*," accessed August 17, 2022, https://www.lexico .com/en/definition/principle.

2 | WHY MODELS MATTER
1. Lexico, s.v. "model, *n.*," accessed August 16, 2022, https://www.lexico .com/en/definition/model.
2. Alan Woodruff, "What Is a Neuron?," Queensland Brain Institute, accessed August 16, 2022, https://qbi.uq.edu.au/brain/brain-anatomy /what-neuron.
3. "Suzana Herculano-Houzel: Neuroscientist," ted.com, accessed March 1, 2021, https://www.ted.com/speakers/suzana_herculano_houzel.

3 | THE BODY NEVER FORGETS
1. I discuss this in my book *The Path out of Loneliness: Finding and Fostering Connection to God, Ourselves, and One Another* (Colorado Springs: NavPress, 2021).

4 | HOW ATTACHMENT AFFECTS OUR EMOTIONS
1. Lexico, s.v. "reciprocity, *n.*," accessed August 16, 2022, https://www .lexico.com/en/definition/reciprocity.
2. Lexico, s.v. "anxious, *adj.*," accessed August 16, 2022, https://www.lexico .com/en/definition/anxious.
3. Lexico, s.v. "avoidant, *adj.*," accessed August 16, 2022, https://www .lexico.com/en/definition/avoidant.

4. Lexico, s.v. "mindset, *n.*," accessed August 16, 2022, https://www.lexico .com/en/definition/mindset.

5. Daniel J. Siegel, *Brainstorm: The Power and Purpose of the Teenage Brain* (New York: Jeremy P. Tarcher/Penguin, 2015), 145–150.

5 | AVOIDANCE IS NEVER THE ANSWER

1. Lexico, s.v. "pain, *n.*," accessed August 17, 2022, https://www.lexico.com /en/definition/pain.

2. Lexico, s.v. "avoidance, *n.*," accessed August 17, 2022, https://www.lexico .com/en/definition/avoidance.

3. Lexico, s.v. "reflex, *n.*," and s.v. "reflex, *adj.*," accessed August 16, 2022, https://www.lexico.com/en/definition/reflex.

4. Lexico, s.v. "stigma, *n.*," accessed August 17, 2022, https://www.lexico .com/en/definition/stigma.

6 | THE IMPORTANCE OF FORGIVENESS

1. Everett L. Worthington Jr., "The Power and Meaning of Forgiveness with Dr. Everett Worthington (podcast)," *Stories of Impact*, June 25, 2021, Templeton World Charity Foundation, https://www.templetonworld charity.org/blog/power-and-meaning-forgiveness-dr-everett-worthington -podcast.

2. Amanda Rowett, "The Freedom of Forgiveness," Bellevue Christian Counseling, June 9, 2015, https://bellevuechristiancounseling.com/ articles/the-freedom-of-forgiveness.

3. Lexico, s.v. "trespass, *v.*," accessed August 17, 2022, https://www.lexico .com/en/definition/trespass.

4. Etymology Dictionary, s.v. "humble, *adj.*," accessed August 16, 2022, https://etymology.en-academic.com/18917/humble.

5. Lexico, s.v. "empathy, *n.*," accessed August 16, 2022, https://www.lexico .com/en/definition/empathy.

6. "Burden of Shame—Letting Go of Shame," Vicky's Forum, accessed August 16, 2022, https://www.vickysforum.com/burden-of -shame-letting-go-of-shame.

7. Mark R. McMinn, *Psychology, Theology, and Spirituality in Christian Counseling* (Carol Stream, IL: Tyndale, 1996), chap. 7.

7 | PAY ATTENTION TO THE TENSION

1. Lexico, s.v. "tension, *n.*," accessed August 17, 2022, https://www.lexico .com/en/definition/tension.

2. Lexico, s.v. "friend, *n.*," accessed August 17, 2022, https://www.lexico.com /en/definition/friend.

3. Lexico, s.v. "perseverance, *n.*," accessed August 17, 2022, https://www.lexico.com/en/definition/perseverance.

4. Lexico, s.v. "patience, *n.*," accessed August 17, 2022, https://www.lexico.com/en/definition/patience.

5. Lexico, s.v. "practice, *n.*," accessed August 17, 2022, https://www.lexico.com/en/definition/practice.

6. Lexico, s.v. "lament, *n.*," accessed August 17, 2022, https://www.lexico.com/en/definition/lament.

8 | ACCEPTANCE IS CRITICAL

1. Lexico, s.v. "acceptance, *n.*," accessed August 17, 2022, https://www.lexico.com/en/definition/acceptance.

2. Lexico, s.v. "recognition, *n.*," accessed August 17, 2022, https://www.lexico.com/en/definition/recognition.

3. Lexico, s.v. "reflection, *n.*," accessed August 17, 2022, https://www.lexico.com/en/definition/reflection.

4. Lexico, s.v. "vulnerability, *n.*," accessed August 17, 2022, https://www.lexico.com/en/definition/vulnerability.

5. Lexico, s.v. "openness, *n.*," accessed August 17, 2022, https://www.lexico.com/en/definition/openness.

9 | A THEOLOGY OF SUFFERING AND CARE

1. Collins Dictionary, s.v. "theology, *n.*," accessed August 17, 2022, https://www.collinsdictionary.com/dictionary/english/theology.

2. Lexico, s.v. "suffering, *n.*," accessed August 17, 2022, https://www.lexico.com/en/definition/suffering.

3. Encyclopedia.com, s.v. "protection, *n.*," accessed August 17, 2022, https://www.encyclopedia.com/social-sciences-and-law/economics-business-and-labor/economics-terms-and-concepts/protection.

4. Lexico, s.v. "care, *n.*," accessed August 17, 2022, https://www.lexico.com/en/definition/care.

5. "What Exactly Is This Thing Called 'Self-Compassion'?," Wildflower Center for Counseling, October 5, 2020, https://www.wildflowercfc.com/post/what-exactly-is-this-thing-called-self-compassion.

10 | DEVELOPING YOUR EMOTIONAL LANGUAGE

1. Lexico, s.v. "language, *n.*," accessed August 17, 2022, https://www.lexico.com/en/definition/language.

2. Lexico, s.v. "meaning, *n.*," accessed August 17, 2022, https://www.lexico.com/en/definition/meaning.

3. Lexico, s.v. "depth, *n.*," accessed August 17, 2022, https://www.lexico.com /en/definition/depth.

4. To access a visual depiction of where these five universal emotions are felt in the body, see Michaeleen Doucleff, "Mapping Emotions on the Body: Love Makes Us Warm All Over," NPR, December 30, 2013, https:// www.npr.org/sections/healthshots/2013/12/30/258313116/mapping -emotions-on-the-body-love-makes-us-warm-all-over.

5. Adapted from the Atlas of Emotions by Paul Ekman and Eve Ekman (2014; http://atlasofemotions.org) and other sources. Copyright © 2017 by Dr. Mark Mayfield. Use with permission only.

6. "Emotion Faces" figure created by Kristina Marcelli-Sargent, LCSW, RPT. To learn more about her work, visit artofsocialwork.com.

NavPress is the book-publishing arm of The Navigators.

Since 1933, The Navigators has helped people around the world bring hope and purpose to others in college campuses, local churches, workplaces, neighborhoods, and hard-to-reach places all over the world, face-to-face and person-by-person in an approach we call Life-to-Life® discipleship. We have committed together to know Christ, make Him known, and help others do the same.®

Would you like to join this adventure of discipleship and disciplemaking?

- Take a Digital Discipleship Journey at **navigators.org/disciplemaking**.
- Get more discipleship and disciplemaking content at **thedisciplemaker.org**.
- Find your next book, Bible, or discipleship resource at **navpress.com**.

 @NavPressPublishing

 @NavPress

 @navpressbooks

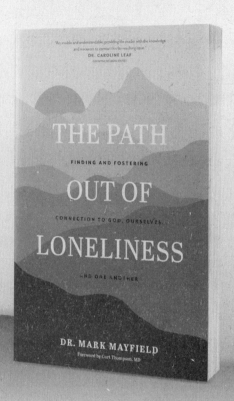